~

THIS GOSPEL PRESENTED TO

_____

BY

_____

~

THE GOSPEL OF ELVIS

THE GOSPEL OF ELVIS

CONTAINING

THE TESTAMENT AND APOCRYPHA
Including all the Greater Themes of the King
WITH AN INTRODUCTION, COMMENTARIES, THE
COMPLETE NOTES OF ST. CLIFF, AND ILLUMINATIONS.

EDITED BY

Solomon B. T. Church, D.R., MSH.

CONSULTING EDITORS

A.L. Ludwig, S.A.M.   G. Izquierdo, S.A.M.

W.F. Ludwig

The Summit Publishing Group, Arlington, Texas

THE SUMMIT PUBLISHING GROUP

Fifth Floor, 1112 East Copeland Road • Arlington, Texas 76011

Published 1995
Printed in the United States of America

99   98   97   96   95   5   4   3   2   1

Library of Congress Cataloging in Publication Data

Cover and Book Design by David Sims

This is a work of reverent fiction.

Similarities between figures in this work and real persons, living or dead, or other figures of reverent fiction, where not coincidental, are meant reverently.

Blessed be the land of Plenty.

∾

St. Kay and St. Tennessee, St. Nora-on-Hennessey,
Sts. George of the Key, Expedite and Ro,
Sts. Jerry and John—The Voice That Said Go,
St. Walt the Only, of the name Walt alone,
J'Ahliba the tax goddess, St. Bruce of the Stone,
St. Louie the Agent, the Secret One true—
I couldn't have done it if it wasn't for you.

—S.B.T. Church

CONTENTS

INTRODUCTION

The Gospel of Elvis is many things, but it is more important to understand what it is not. *The Gospel of Elvis* does not claim Elvis Presley to be God, a god, a son or Son of God, a messenger of God or the gods, greater than or equal to Jesus, Moses, Mohammed, Buddha, Krishna, or any other religious figure. Nor does the *Gospel* claim to be an accurate or complete history of Elvis Presley and his times.

This is a story, and a very funny story at that. It is filled with great jokes and terrible puns, and not a little revealed truth about religion, power, and rock and roll.

It borrows liberally from the Bible and several histories of Elvis Presley, as well as many other less controversial sources, but it is not those stories.

It is the tale of a messiah. Not the Messiah, for his tale has already been told, but still a man, born in a humble village to a pure-hearted mother, anointed and proclaimed King, whose destiny was to liberate his land from the grip of a coldhearted, spiritless invader and save his people's soul. It is also the story of that people, and a brief time in their history when all seemed possible and nothing was too great to dream, even freedom.

If this story sounds a bit familiar, don't be surprised. You might have heard something like it once on the radio . . .

PROLOGUE

The year is 1945 and the old world has been destroyed by war. In its place a new World is rising, defined by Hollywood and Madison Avenue, filled with new cars and tidy, suburban homes, a clean, wholesome place, sanitized for convenience and untouched by human hands.

Underneath the surface of this shiny, new World, however, are stirring forces of discontent and change. The war has forever altered the relationships between the sexes, and the races as well. The postwar boom brings an unprecedented freedom and affluence to the young. Conflicts are growing that, in less than a decade, will blow the lid off of America, and the World it has made.

The fuse would be supplied by a young man raised far from that gleaming World, back in the mud and pines where America grew up. He loved God, his mama and any kind of music, black, white, sacred or profane, so long as it moved him. That love of song, regardless of style, forged a man who would combine in himself all of America's opposites, a new and powerful Voice that would set World on its ear, the man who would be the King.

"It all seemed to make sense at the time."

∽

GENESIS

1 In the beginning was the War and the War was with God and the War was God. And God saw that it was good.

2 War was the end of everything and the beginning of nothing, and the prophets of nothing were not gladdened to proclaim "I told you so." War smote all of the seven pillars and all of the seven wonders and all of the seven hills and in the burning of all the world's sevens was brought forth World.

1 *"the War"—World War II.*

2 *"the prophets of nothing"—Postwar existentialists Jean Paul Sartre and Albert Camus. "World"—the idealized, homogenous image of American culture that dominated the world following W.W.II.*

3 *"Beaver"—Baby Boom-era American boy, personified by "Beaver" Cleaver, lead character in the television show* Leave it to Beaver.

4 *"the trials before"—the Great Depression. "the fathers of Beaver"—adult American male, c. 1946-1976. Here the identification of World with a capital W with American popular culture is reinforced, as distinct from the mundane world.*

5 *"the green part of the earth"—the Western Hemisphere. "Plenty"—the United States.*

3 And out of the dust of War, God made the first man, Beaver, and into him breathed the breath of life. And Beaver saw that it was not so good.

4 War and the trials before had made the fathers of Beaver into slaves, and across the face of the world stretched World.

5 By the will of World were the fathers of Beaver taken from him, and he was placed in a garden in the green part of the earth, that place which was called Plenty, where the war had been won, but never fought, and World had been born.

6 Beaver wept.

7 When the mother of Beaver told the fathers of Beaver of the child's unhap-

piness alone in the garden, the fathers of Beaver gave unto the mother of Beaver a Radio, saying "Give unto the child this day this Radio. From it shall he hear Voices, from which he shall see visions, and he shall believe the Voices to be the voices of his fathers and be happy." And Beaver saw that it was good.

Again, World is shown to be something other than the earth.

6 *Like John 11:35, this is the Gospel's shortest verse.*

7 *"Radio"— American radio programming, particularly network music programming. The passage that follows in "Luke 1" bolsters this interpretation.*

LUKE

1 In those days World made the Radio in his own image. Male and female created he Radio, but in one color only. World feared the Voices of the hot, dark people of Plenty and denied them radio. For the Voices of the hot, dark people there was radio, but World decreed that only the sad Voices of the cold, light people would be heard on *the* Radio.

1 *"Voices"—recording artists/pop stars. The verse recalls the difficulty black artists encountered in getting airplay on network radio in the forties and fifties, being relegated to the independent stations and disc jockeys who were allowed late-night shows featuring "race records."*

2 *"Luke"—Hank Williams, who was "so lonesome I could cry."*

2 Amidst the Voices Beaver heard and believed to be his fathers was one so lonesome he Cried in the wilderness. Many who heard this man, who was called Luke, thought him to be the king that would deliver the children of Plenty from the wilderness of Radio.

3 *"sweet lies of strings"—either a reference to orchestral ballads by singers like Sinatra and Crosby, or a comment on Owen Bradley's signature production sound exemplified by his recordings of Patsy Cline.*

3 Why did the people of Plenty believe Luke to be the prophesied King? He was, after all, just a man, and only one of the Voices of the cold, light people. Still, among them, he was the first to have any of the powers of the hot, dark people: Luke could Cry. Other Voices sang of hearts broken and love lost forever, but Beaver knew they lied sweet lies

of strings. Luke wandered with nothing but his voice, broken and dry as the desert, and none who heard him doubted that he Cried.

4 When World heard Luke Crying, he was made afraid, for he knew that, though Crying was the least of the powers of the hot, dark people, Luke was a danger to World's dominion. Therefore did World cause Luke to be overpowered by a sleep curse and made to drift from his throne in the back seat.

4 *"overpowered by a sleep curse . . . in the back seat"—On January 1, 1953, Williams was found dead of a drug overdose in the back of his Cadillac.*

BROTHER

1 Another of the true fathers of Beaver was called Brother. He too had the power to Cry, though he hid it, seeing what World had done to Luke. Brother instead put on the mask of the Voices of the cold, light people, and made light of his powers, calling those in his sect In-sects and his followers kids.

2 So clever was Brother's disguise that he was allowed to walk in the land of Plenty for many years and his voice was

1 *"Brother"—Buddy Holly. "In-sects"—Holly's band The Crickets.*

2 *"the home of the hot, dark people"—the Apollo Theater in Harlem.*

heard throughout the land, swaying the people of Plenty, for he brought to the Radio the greatest of the powers of the hot, dark people: the power to Shake. So great were Brother's powers that he was able to stand in the home of the hot, dark people and Shake, and they saw that it was good. All of this Brother was able to do without raising the suspicion of World or the fathers of Beaver.

3 And the people of Plenty were sore amazed, and asked Brother if he were the king sent to deliver them from the wilderness, but Brother, remembering the fate of Luke, replied he was only an In-sect. Still World, seeing the power of Brother, was made afraid, and

caused Brother to be locked in the great prison city called Empire in the east of Plenty, until he could decide what to do about him.

4 Brother would not be kept in the prison city, though, and used his powers to fly into the West, hoping to meet again with the In-sects in the Great Carnival. World, however, descried Brother's flight and reached out to pick him from the air like a cricket.

5 Beaver saw that it was getting very bad.

3 *"city called Empire"* — *New York.*

4 *Refers to the February 3, 1959 plane crash during the Winter Carnival tour, which took the lives of Holly, Richie Valens ("La Bamba") and the Big Bopper ("Chantilly Lace").*

COYOTE CALLS

1 Among the Voices of the Radio, were the voices which called the Voices, who were called the horsemen. They called upon the Voices to sing for Beaver and the Voices sang. Among these were some whose power of calling was so great that they were said to have become Voices themselves, and the greatest among these great horsemen was Coyote.

2 Long before the legend of the Wolf grew in the West, long before the mighty

1 *"horsemen"—disc jockeys. "great horsemen"—Early rock and roll DJs often achieved a star status on their own through wild antics and nonstop "jive" patter. "Coyote"—Cleveland DJ Alan "Moondog" Freed.*

2 *"the Wolf"—Wolfman Jack. "Healer Father*

and Father Ender . . . Old City at the mouth of the Great Middle River"—New Orleans disc jockeys Dr. Daddy-O and Poppa Stoppa. "the City of Steel . . . River of Slag"—as Pittsburgh is most commonly called the "Iron City," the author uses the image of a "City of Steel" here to emphasize the industrial character of Cleveland.

3 "the clan of Target"—This is the only direct reference in The Gospel of Elvis to the Jewish people and emphasizes two of the three images gentile Ameri-

calls of the Healer Father and Father Ender were heard in Old City at the mouth of the Great Middle River, Coyote called in the City of Steel, beneath the iron bridges of the River of Slag.

3 Coyote feared not the power of World, nor any other thing, for he was of the clan of Target. The Targets had been tested sorely throughout the history of the world, and had been of the most precious sevens smashed in the war that made World. The few who had survived were said to be invulnerable to all magic except the spells of their own mothers.

4 Coyote lived in Steel City, working by day selling the frozen voice-pictures of the hot, dark people. When night

fell and the moon rose, Coyote would climb the mountain above his lair with his voice-pictures and call the Voices from the air. His calling was so powerful that the radio where he called the Voices of the hot, dark people was like unto Radio itself, and World was powerless against him.

5 And lo, the power of Coyote's calling was so great that the hot, dark people came from all over the City of Steel and all the lands surrounding to buy the frozen voice-pictures. Night after night, the brothers and sisters of Beaver joined the hot, dark children, alone in their beds with the glowing radios, listening to Coyote howl as the

cans most identify with Jews: the Holocaust and the Jewish mother.

4 "voice-pictures"—phonograph records. While Freed didn't actually sell records, he heavily promoted discs for the Record Rendezvous store on his WJW radio program, "Moondog House."

5 "rock and roll"—Freed is credited with the creation of the phrase, but in truth he pulled it out of the "rock" jive on the Bill Haley record "Rock-a-Beat-in' Boogie."

hot, dark Voices poured down on the city like rain. And Coyote howled, "There is one who cometh, whose voice shall be greater than any Voice, and His name shall be called Rock and Roll."

6 World watched with growing concern as Coyote's howls echoed across the Valley of Steel. Still, World waited, for Coyote broke not World's law, but sold the frozen voice-pictures only to the hot, dark people.

7 Then Coyote called for the Jamboree.

6 *"World's law"—racial segregation, official or tacit.*

THE JAMBOREE

1 Rock and roll would arrive and be crowned. The masters of the voice-pictures of the hot, dark people would come in person to call. The power of the Voices would push down the walls that imprisoned the hot, dark people and the land would Shake.

2 This World could not allow. He acted quickly, spreading rumors of death and mayhem among the fathers of Beaver, so that none would allow the cold, white

Despite the title, this section has nothing to do with the Jamboree held at Cleveland's Circle Theater, where Elvis played in February of 1955. From the context, it's clear that this is the story of the "Moondog Coronation Ball," a concert Freed attempted to promote at the Cleveland Arena, March 21, 1952. The concert, featuring "masters of

the voice-pic-
tures" Paul
Williams and
the Huckle-
buckers, Tony
Grimes and the
Rockin' High-
landers, the
Dominoes,
Danny Cobb
and Varetta
Dillard, had
hardly begun
before it turned
into a full-
scale riot, rock
and roll's first.

children near the Jamboree. Then he reached deep into his power and cast the greatest of his curses on Coyote, the curse of race, so that neither the cold, light people nor the hot, dark people would call him their own.

3 So it was that on the day of the Jamboree, the multitudes of hot, dark people came to the City of Steel and claimed the Jamboree for themselves, casting out Coyote and his cold, light brothers. "See," cried World to the fathers of Beaver, "this is a madness of the dark ones. Come no closer or they shall turn on you as well." And the fathers of Beaver shook their heads gravely.

4 But something had changed with

the Jamboree. The cold, white children had listened from afar and heard Coyote's call to Shake. Louder and faster came the Voices, light and dark together on the Radio—the Duck, the Big Man, the Fat Man. But it was not until the eleventh year since War had created World that Astronomer came forth and told Beaver and the brothers and sisters of Beaver what time it was. Rock and roll had arrived, and He would be called King.

5 But He came not from the City of Steel, nor Old City of the Great Middle River, nor the city of Empire in the East, nor the city of Heaven in the West. He came from the very heart of the dark, southern land, a land defeated in a war

4 *"the Duck"—Chuck Berry, after his trademark "duckwalk." "the Big Man"—"Big Joe" Turner. "the Fat Man"—Antoine "Fats" Domino. "the Astronomer"—Bill Haley, who, with his band the Comets, "told Beaver what time it was" with the song "Rock Around the Clock,"* featured in the film The Blackboard Jungle.

5 *"the city of Heaven"—Los Angeles. "Grandfather War"—American Civil War.*

which was grandfather to War, a land ridiculed in all the great cities of Plenty. There, in the humblest house in the smallest village of Plenty, was born the King.

THE COMING OF THE KING

1 In the times of the trials, before War made World, the world sensed its coming death and sent through the dark clouds of the trials shards of its spirit, which were born as human children to the children of the world, to sustain them when the world was no more.

2 In those days Caesar Patricius of Plenty caused to be held a levy of all the people of the world, so that from each could be taken according to his ability,

1 *See C.G. Jung,* Answer to Job, *for an analysis of the concept of the "shards" of God's spirit.*

2 *See Luke 2:1. "Caesar Patricius of Plenty"—F. D. Roosevelt.*

and each should know his place.

3 Therefore were found in the village of Dog's Tree in the hottest, darkest corner of the southern part of Plenty, Goodman Green King Before and his wife, who was named Love. Green King and Love were decent, hard-working people whom the world loved, and so the world sent two shards of its spirit to grow in the womb of Love, and said, "Beloved are you, Love, for you shall give birth to the two greatest of Voices, Kingson and Kingsfather, and you shall be called Sacred Mama."

4 But the spirit of World was already stirring in the shadow places of the world, and sent two poisoned bolts

3 *"Dog's Tree"—Elvis's birthplace of Tupelo, Mississippi. A tupelo is a variety of dogwood tree. "Goodman Green King Before"—Vernon Presley, Elvis's father. "Love"— Gladys Love Presley, Elvis's mother. "Kingson" —Elvis Aron Presley. "Kingsfather"—Jesse Garon Presley, Elvis's stillborn twin brother.*

to kill the sons of Green King and Love in the womb of Love. The world tried to save the sons of Love, but one of the bolts hit home and slew Kingsfather as the children were born. The shard of the spirit of the world that was Kingsfather was swallowed by the baby Kingson as He drew breath for His first cry, and He became King.

5 Even as a child in Dog's Tree, the King was hailed as an anointed one. Early in His youth, He was known for His singing and His love of the Sacred Mama Love. It is remembered that He was called as a child to sing at a gathering of farmers in Dog's Tree, and He sang them a simple country song their fathers had

4 *"the spirit . . . was swallowed by the baby Kingson"*— Gladys Presley believed that Elvis acquired his dead twin's strength.

5 *"sang them a simple country song"*—reference to Elvis's performance of the country tearjerker "Old Shep" at the Mississippi-Alabama Fair, October 3, 1945.

wept to. The people of Dog's Tree began to call Him a Voice.

6 The King walked the streets of Dog's Tree, confused and frightened. He did not want to be a Voice. He wanted to be a normal boy. It was then that World placed before the King His first temptation, the gun. A shining steel vision behind the polished glass of a shop window, the gun whispered to the King of the joys a normal boy could learn—the pride of the hunter, the terrifying power of the soldier. He went home and told Sacred Mama Love of the glorious gun. He knew that His birthfest was coming, on Fourteenth Night, and pleaded with Sacred Mama Love that He might own the gun.

7 Sacred Mama Love went to see the gun, and she saw that it was World's temptation, and she prayed for her son. Then the ghost of the world whispered to her to look deeper within the shop, and there she saw a guitar.

8 She brought the guitar home to the King and said, "This shall be your weapon, my son." And the King took the guitar and pledged, "With this weapon, I shall conquer the world for you, Mama," and Sacred Mama Love knew she had saved the King from World's curse and the life of a normal boy.

9 The King knew it too, for He loved His Sacred Mama, and would do her will in everything. Still, the vision of

the gun was not easily scrubbed from
His eyes.

THE SHRINE OF FATHER SAM

1 Green King and Love moved to Mud City north of Dog's Tree, and the King grew. Living and working among the hot, dark people, He learned their ways and was taught the mysteries of Crying and Shaking. He, too, heard the nightly call of the Voices on the Radio and learned from each a new power.

2 By the time He was a young man, working as a teamster, He was known in Mud City as a Voice, and an extraordinary

*1-2 "Mud City"
—Memphis,
Tennessee.
Growing up in
Memphis, Elvis
was exposed to
a wealth of mu-
sical styles,
from white and
black spiritual
music to blues
to country and
hillbilly. De-
spite a nearly
crippling shy-
ness, Elvis
began singing
at fairs, con-
certs and talent
shows while
working as a
truck driver.*

2 *"Priest-King" —On April 9, 1953, Elvis played guitar in a show with the L.C. Humes HS band, billed as "Elvis Prestly." "Eldest King"—In the summer of 1954, Elvis performed at the Overton Park Shell under the billing "Ellis Presley."*

3-4 *"Father Sam's shrine"—Sun Records, 706 Union Avenue in Memphis, was founded and managed by Sam Phillips, whom many credit with bringing together the black Delta blues and the white hillbilly sound to make rock and roll.*

Voice He was. He had merged within Himself the powers of the Voices of the hot, dark people and their cold, light cousins. His reputation grew, though no one would proclaim Him king openly. At gatherings of singers in Mud City, they would refer to Him as "Priest-King" or "Eldest King." Each time He would reply, "I am only a Mama's son" and sing them the simple hill songs that their fathers had wept to.

3 It was decided to bring Him to be tested at Father Sam's shrine.

4 In Mud City, in the shrine kept by Father Sam, stood a microphone. Father Sam believed that, if he prayed and faithfully tended the shrine, the ghost of

St. Luke would guide him to the King. Father Sam prayed and prayed, and Voices gathered around him—the Black Man and the Murderer, St. Crispin and the Lonely Man.

5 And lo, the King came among them, a young man, and sang for them the songs of the hot, dark people. Father Sam heard Him and was amazed, for even as one so young, the King had the power of St. Luke to Cry. But by then so many had that power, even the one called White Buck. Father Sam asked the King what other powers He had. The King prayed to the spirit of Sacred Mama. He felt her presence descend and proclaimed "That was

4 "St. Luke"— Hank Williams. "the Black Man"— Johnny Cash ("The Man in Black"). "the Murderer"— Jerry Lee Lewis, nick-named "Killer." "St. Crispin"— Carl Perkins, who wrote "Blue Suede Shoes" in 1955. St. Crispin is the patron saint of shoemakers. "the Lonely Man"—Roy Orbison.

5 "White Buck"—Pat Boone. "That was alright"—"That's Alright, Mama" was recorded in Sun Studios in the summer of 1954 and released on the Sun label July 19, 1954.

alright." And Father Sam heard Him and cried, "He Shakes!"

6 And the Voices and Father Sam turned to the King, awaiting the next song. But the King could sing no more. And the ghost of St. Luke hovered over the city, saying, "He is already more than I ever was, but He is not ready."

7 The King resumed His life as a teamster, but began going to gatherings throughout the hot, southern lands with His men, who would make the beginnings of His court. Wherever He went He would Shake, and Beaver and his countless sisters would come and be Shaken. The sisters of Beaver would swoon and foam, weeping and rending

their garments. It was said He could send His voice in a way that only women could hear, and that when they heard the King's voice, they had no choice but to obey His call.

8 Then, in the beginning of the year following the Astronomer's Year, the King made a pilgrimage to the shrine in the city of St. Luke. He spoke few words as He stood before the microphone at the St. Luke shrine. Around Him gathered the spirits of the Voices of the shrine, above Him floated the spirit of St. Luke, and there He revealed the power that made Him King: He could Die.

9 Around Him knelt the spirits of all the Voices, living and dead, crying, "Let us

8 "the Astronomer's Year"—1955, the year Bill Haley and His Comets released "Rock Around the Clock." "the city of St. Luke"—Nashville, Tennessee. "the St. Luke shrine"—From the context, the RCA Building at 30 Music Square West in Nashville. "The power... he could Die"—On the surface a reference to Elvis's biggest record, "Heartbreak Hotel," recorded at RCA's Nashville studio January 5, 1956. For more on the image of the dead-and-resurrected king, see Joseph Campbell, The

Hero with a Thousand Faces; *Sir James Frazer,* The Golden Bough; *and Baigent, et al.,* Holy Blood, Holy Grail, *particularly chapter 12: "The Priest-King Who Never Ruled." Compare with John 11:1-46.*

Die, also, that He may raise us up," and above floated the spirit of St. Luke, crying, "Behold my son—He is ready."

THE LORD MAYORS

1 When the King Died and was raised up at the shrine, Father Sam caused to be made voice-pictures to be sent throughout the land of Plenty to announce the coming of the King. Soon, processions were planned to take the King through the hot, southern lands. The plans grew until it was clear that the King and Green King could not manage it all and a lord mayor must be appointed for the King's retinue.

1 "lord mayor"— manager.

2 "Increase"— Scotty Moore, Elvis's lead guitarist from the earliest days at Sun Studios until 1968, was also the King's first manager, from July 1954 until January 1, 1955, when disc jockey/promoter Bob Neal ("Normal the Famous") took over.

"specter"—producer. Moore is often credited with helping create and define Elvis's early sound. "ghost-voice"—session player or backup vocalist.

4 "Normal the Famous"—WMPS disc jockey Bob Neal. The name "Normal" is presumably given to emphasize the difference between Neal, by all accounts an honest and likable fellow, and Colonel Tom Parker. "Year of the Dog"—1956, the year

2 The first lord mayor was the one named Increase, though he was called the King's specter. A ghost-voice in the shrine of Father Sam, Increase was one of the first called to the King, and would Shake and Cry and Die with Him. Increase knew of the King's powers and rituals, and also saw the power the King would wield in the land of Plenty and beyond.

3 Before long, however, Increase knew the task was too great for him. He went to the King and said, "I would remain to Shake with thee and Cry with thee and Die with thee, but I cannot remain thy lord mayor, for soon thy kingdom shall be of all the lands. Thou must find a true lord mayor and let me be thy specter again."

4 Though the King argued with him, He knew Increase was right, and called upon Normal the Famous, a horseman in Mud City, who agreed to be the King's lord mayor. Normal served loyally throughout the Year of the Astronomer and into the spring of the Year of the Dog, as the King went on procession and sent voice-pictures throughout the land.

5 In the hottest, southernmost part of Plenty, there is a land called Waterland, because there it is so wet one cannot draw the line between sky and water. There, where ruled Freon the Mighty, the King met the Snake.

"Hound Dog" was released. See "The City of Empire 5."

5 "Waterland"— Florida. The author sets Elvis's first meeting with Colonel Tom Parker ("the Snake") at the Gator Bowl show in Jacksonville in May 1953. In actuality, the Colonel had been watching Elvis for months, waiting to lock the promising young star into a management contract. Even before officially becoming Elvis's manager on March 15, 1956, Parker had already been sharing management duties with Neal.

THE SNAKE

1 When He shook at the shrine in Mud City, the King was known to the world and to World. When the King died and His star was born at the shrine in the city of St. Luke, World knew the King must die the true death. Then might World take over the soul of the King and make a golem of Him.

2 Many were the tools at hand, forged in the fires of War and War's father, War, and quenched in the cold

1 *"true death"—bodily death, as opposed to the ritual death in "The Shrine of Father Sam 8."*

2 *"War's father, War"—World War I.*

emptiness of the trials between. Among them all, World chose the Snake.

3 "the Land of a Thousand Years"—Germany. "giants" —Hitler, Stalin, Mussolini. "the Old Lands"—Europe. "gold by alchemy" — reference to the wild financial speculation in America during the late 1920s.

3 When War the Father had left the old part of the world, the trials began at once in the dust of the Land of a Thousand Years, long before they touched the shores of Plenty. As the trials deepened and the dust began to form the giants who would fight War the Son, many fled the Old Lands to the promise of Plenty. Plenty seemed to float untouched above the world. While she had spent countless sons in tribute to War the Father, her own wide spaces remained green and virgin, so unlike the scorched graveyards that were once the gentle Old Lands. While the rest of the

world traded old empires for coarse bread, the people of Plenty seemed to be making gold by alchemy.

4 In the Year the Alchemists' Spells Failed and the trials came, the Snake crossed the sea to the land of Plenty. He immediately sought the dark hollows where a snake might live. Soon he moved south to the hot, wet lands where a snake would thrive. War the Father and the trials had taught him that living was more important than right or wrong and that living meant stealing. When the Snake found himself among the cold, light people of the dark, southern lands of Plenty, he disguised himself as one of them, and grew fat stealing from them. He loved

4 *"the year the Alchemists' spells failed"* In 1929, Parker emigrated to America from the Netherlands. *"dark hollows"*— West Virginia.

befriending them and gaining their confidence, then taking from them all they had. Seeing the coming of War the Son and World, the Snake knew he had been wise to come to Plenty.

5 Then came World to the Snake saying, "Thou hast become truly a son of World, and beloved. Thou shalt be my glory and my sword hand and reign over the King who reigneth over all. Wilt thou do the bidding of World and receive World's blessing?" And the Snake answered, "You bet." And World blessed the Snake, saying, "Behold, you shall have the power to steal half of all the wealth of the King, but you must kill Him also." And the Snake answered, "No problem."

HALF A KINGDOM

1 So the Snake left the mummer's show where he tortured cocks for fairgoers and sought out the King's procession in the northernmost village of Waterland. Finding the King as He left a gathering, the Snake challenged Him.

2 "You, who call yourself King!" cried the Snake, "where is your kingdom? You are but a Voice, Crying in the wilderness. What sort of lord mayor have you, who drags you through the swamps

1 *"mummer's show . . . tortured cocks for fairgoers"*—a carnival huckster and inveterate con man, Parker once had an act called Col. Parker and His Dancing Chickens, who would indeed dance when Parker turned on a hot plate under the chickens' stage. *"northernmost village of Waterland"* — Jacksonville.

2 *"Babylon of the Golden Desert"—Las Vegas, Nevada.*

3 *"caller"—disc jockey. "chariot"—Cadillac.*

of Waterland when a King should be crowned in the city of Empire, or the city of Heaven, or Babylon of the Golden Desert?"

3 "How has this caller increased your kingdom in this fateful year? If only you'd had a real lord mayor working for you, one who was wise in the ways of World, you would already be King in truth, not just in name, with the wealth of the world spread out before you. Yours would be the chariot of gold and the house on the hill. Your Sacred Mama would be riding a pink chariot instead of bouncing through Mud City in Green King's wagon."

4 The courtiers were struck dumb

by the Snake's words, for none had ever talked to the King thus, but the King did not protest. The Snake's words seemed to strike Him like a closed fist, yet beckon and shine like the gun He had coveted as a child in Dog's Tree, for World had opened unto the Snake the deepest fears and temptations of the young King, and the Snake was not loath to use what powers he might to bind the King.

5 Entranced as He was, the King was not beguiled, and asked the Snake what such a lord mayor would require for his services. "Half a kingdom," the Snake replied with cold, unmoving eyes.

6 "Half a kingdom!" cried the courtiers. "Incredible! A jest!" Normal

5 *"Half a kingdom"*—*Parker's eventual contract with Elvis was a nominal fifty-fifty split of all income. With creative expense accounting and charging fees to songwriters, scriptwriters, etc., it is widely believed Parker made much more than Elvis from the King's career.*

the Famous pleaded with the King, "Majesty, do not do this thing. This reptile promises you the World in your hand but I fear it shall be the other way around."

7 Laughing, the Snake taunted the King: "See how he seeks to save his little piece of a kingdom of Mud, rather than see you rule a whole world."

8 "Only half a World it seems," noted the King. "Tell me, Scaled One, can you truly assure my coronation in the city of Empire?" The Snake answered: "Before the year is out, Your Greatness."

9 But Increase did not trust the Snake and said, "Majesty, he speaks with forked tongue."

10 "Fit, to be called liar by a lyre-man," said the Snake. "And fit that a king of Mud should have for subjects mud-toed peasants. A pity, though. What might your empire be, run by a real man of the World."

11 "Or a real Snake in the grass," said the King. "Reptile, you shall have a chance to make good your boasts. Henceforth you shall be my lord mayor with license to run this kingdom as you see fit, for half of the wealth therein. At such time as I find fault with your stewardship, or simply grow weary of you, you shall be banished from me and no part of me shall you know, with neither treasure nor the power of my Name to

10 *"lyreman"*— *guitarist.*

save you from your beloved World."

12 Smiling a lipless, scaled smile, the Snake spoke one word only: "Deal."

THE CITY OF EMPIRE

1 And so it followed as the Snake had prophesied. Within a moon, Sacred Mama rode through the streets of Mud City in a new pink chariot and the courtiers prepared for the caravan to the city of Empire.

2 The King asked the Snake if they were going for His coronation. The Snake laughed. "All pardons, Majesty, but the people of Plenty will not accept you as King yet. There are signs and proofs that

Both the chronology and the geography of this period are scrambled. "Hound Dog," etc. were all recorded at RCA's New York studios on 24th Street, after the television appearances with Berle and Allen. See "The Inquisition."

3 *"City of the Radio… first shrine of the voices"*—Radio City. *"Stone Man Square"*—Rockefeller Center. *"St. George"*—George West-inghouse. *"St. Nikola"*—Nikola Tesla.

4 *"Faust"*—Frank Sinatra, made clear in *"The Contest with Faust."* It is uncertain whether the reference is to Sinatra's *"dev-ilish"* luck with women or the rumors of a *"pact"* between him and orga-nized crime.

must be fulfilled. We journey now to one of your trials."

3 "In the heart of the city of Empire is another tiny city, the City of the Radio. It is a city of temples which together make up the first shrine of the Voices, marked on the city plan as Stone Man Square. Its true name is the Shrine of St. George and St. Nikola but do not use this name among laymen nor in the shrine itself."

4 "The power of this shrine is so great that it has been known to burn singers to their deaths. Faust himself was made before its sacred microphone. Majesty, if you can stand in the first shrine of the Voices in the City of the

THE CITY OF EMPIRE

Radio and Die without dying, they shall have no choice but to crown you King in the city of Empire."

5 So the King and His court, along with the choir from the Shrine of St. Luke, rode the caravan to the city of Empire and gathered around the microphone in the City of the Radio. And there the King astounded them, singing a simple peasant's love song. The Snake thought He had gone mad. Then, as the King sang, He began to Shake, and all around the microphone Shook also, and the whole shrine and the city beyond Shook with the power of the King. Then, with a special dedication to the Snake, the King proclaimed the Year of the Dog.

5 *"choir of the Shrine of St. Luke" —The Jordanaires. "peasant's love song... Year of the Dog"—either "Don't Be Cruel" or "Anyway You Want Me (That's How I'll Be)," both recorded July 2,1956, along with "Hound Dog."*

6 *"Old One"— the Devil. See "The Cross of Light," "Golgotha."*

6 Voice-pictures from the shrine, naming the year, went out to all the horsemen of Plenty, and the horsemen called. Though there was no message from Faust, nor from the Old One in Babylon, none doubted who was King in the city of Empire.

THE INQUISITION

1 The King was crowned before a live audience at the picture-radio gathering of the prophet WoMan in the city of Empire. When the multitudes saw Him Shake on the picture-radio, He drove them to frenzy. The fathers of Beaver were afraid of the effect He had on their daughters, their wives.

2 At that time the leader of Plenty was a hero of Almighty War called the Bald One. Though he was a good man

1 *"picture-radio gathering"— television show. "WoMan"— Milton Berle.*

2 *"the Bald One"—Dwight D. Eisenhower.*

"Sharers"—
communists.
"the Inquisi-
tion"—the
"Red Scare"
anti-commu-
nism of the
fifties.

himself, under him festered a thousand ministers and offices, many not part of the government proper, all with the duty of finding and exposing Sharers, or any other citizens of Plenty who would weaken the morals and loyalty of their fellow Plentians. Singly, each was a tiny picture of World, and didn't know it. Together they made up the Inquisition, and no one was above them.

3 *"the Court of*
the Good
Joe"—Senate
investigative
panel chaired
by Sen. Joseph
McCarthy.

3 The fathers of Beaver approached the mysterious officers of the Inquisition and begged them to call the King before the Court of the Good Joe. The officers told the fathers that they could not bring the King before the Good Joe lest they prove Him a Sharer, but that they might

count on the lesser offices of the Inquisition to help them bring down the threat to their wives and daughters.

4 Committees were formed, and shadow-pictures were made denouncing the King and warning of the evils of Shaking. Calls went forth to ban the King from the Radio. Quickly the King appeared again on the picture-radio with the prophet known as Smock, who was beloved in Plenty, but the Inquisition pressed on, even using the forbidden word-spell "sex" referring to the King.

5 Finally, the Snake went to the prophet called the Big Showman, whose Sabbath picture-radio gathering was attended so regularly by so many in

4 *"shadow-pictures"—films. "Smock"— Steve Allen.*

5 *"the Big Showman"—Ed Sullivan.*

Plenty that it was as Caeser's church. The Snake begged the Big Showman to bring forth the King, and acknowledge Him, and the Showman agreed, proclaiming the King a "real decent fine boy" and "thoroughly alright." The Big Showman was so beloved in Plenty that the Inquisition could not gainsay him.

THE YEAR OF THE SHAKING

1 The King returned to Mud City and, as the Snake had foretold, moved to a palace on a hill which He named the Residence of Mercy, and rode about in a chariot of gold. He showered Sacred Mama and Green King as well as the men of His court and the ladies in waiting with gold and gifts. He would then have been content to remain in Mud City, among the people He knew and loved, but the Snake told Him there were new

The title is a reference to Jerry Lee Lewis's "Whole Lotta Shakin Goin' On," which was released in 1957. See verse 5: "The Murderer said it aloud."

1 *"Residence of Mercy"— Graceland.*

trials to be endured before He could be crowned King of all Plenty.

2 The Snake brought Him in a conquering procession to the city of Heaven in the West, where the great kings of shadow-picture bowed before Him.

3 "Great art thou, oh King," they proclaimed. "We pray thee, let us make shadow-pictures of thee for the multitudes to adore."

4 And the King knew from the Snake that this was how kings were made in the city of Heaven, as the Snake knew from World that this was how kings were tamed and broken to the will of World. So He made their shadow-pictures, tales of love and unjust punishment, stories so

simple as to insult the lowest village idiot of Plenty, but when the King sang, they seemed the greatest stories ever told, and when the King Shook, all in Heaven Shook with Him.

5 All of Plenty Shook that year. The Murderer said it aloud, back in the shrine of Father Sam, but by then there was only one King in Plenty, and all others were only Voices.

6 The King rode in fewer and fewer processions, for soon the multitudes of Plenty were coming to him, among them women seeking to be the King's bride or His concubine. There were women unnumbered, from the most powerful princesses of Empire and Heaven to the

lowest serving maids, all craving the touch of the King. And the King did His royal best to touch them all.

7 The Snake began to be afraid for the King. The Snake knew the people of Plenty toppled their kings before for such things, for such was the power of World in Plenty that, though all knew of the great power of sex, none might speak of it directly, nor be seen in its presence. The persecutions of the Murderer and the Duck had proved that.

8 Something, thought the Snake, must be done.

7 *"The persecutions of the Murderer and The Duck" - Both Jerry Lee Lewis and Chuck Berry got in trouble with underage girls, Lewis snuffing his career in its cradle, so to speak, by marrying his thirteen-year-old cousin, and Berry serving two years under the Mann Act.*

THE WARRIOR KING

1 The following year, the Year of John the Good and John of the Birch, the Snake came to the King, saying, "Majesty, you must have thought for the fathers of Beaver, for you sin greatly in their eyes." "What do I care what those World-loving fathers think?" the King proudly scoffed, but the Snake continued: "Wise men know that the King is above mortal standards of sin, but a wise king would not ignore them. You are not

1 "Year of John the Good / John of the Birch"— 1958, when Chuck Berry's "Johnny B. Goode" was released and the John Birch Society was founded.

so strong that the fathers of Beaver can't break you yet."

2 "To many you are a devil, to many a simple singer, probably a man-lover and a Sharer to boot. You still cannot be trusted or loved by the multitudes of Plenty, these fathers of Beaver and children of the Bald One. You have one more trial, Majesty, the hardest of all."

3 "For two years you must cease Shaking and Crying and Dying. There will be no shadow-pictures, no voice-pictures, no Radio. You must enter the army of Plenty as a common soldier and fight the Sharing Empire in the crusade for the New Land of a Thousand Years."

4 The King protested. He must not

3 *"Sharing Empire"* —communism. *"the New Land of a Thousand Years"*— West Germany.

stop making shadow-pictures and voice-pictures now. Pretenders to the throne lurked everywhere, watching the King's every move to see how a King held Himself—the Duck, the Comb with his own picture-radio gathering, that street kid from the city of Empire.

5 The Snake chastised Him: "Foolish Majesty! The king of shadow-pictures and the king of picture-radio are kings of now. You must be crowned King of Always. This you cannot do until you win the hearts of the fathers of Beaver, who control the wealth and power of Plenty."

6 "The fathers have no holier holy than War. The spirit-war they play with the Sharers is nothing more than an

4 *"the Comb"*— *Ricky Nelson.* *"that street kid"* —*Dion.*

6 *"spirit-war,"* *"crusade"*

endless homage to War. But do not mock this crusade, for it is the cornerstone of Plenty in these days, and none who will not stand against the Sharers shall ever be King in Plenty. The phantom servants of the Bald One and the Good Joe will make sure of it."

7 The King was unhappy with the plan. He had a dim vision of Sacred Mama Love, and she was taking a dim vision of it also. The Snake poured a libation and cast a spell: "To War the Spirit, Son of War the Son. We must show them you are not just a Cryer and a Shaker and a Dying faker, but a warrior king, pledged to the sacred gun."

8 At the invocation of the gun, the Snake knew he had turned the heart of the

King, who ignored the vision of His Sacred Mama and bowed instead to the vision of shining, deadly steel. The King raised no more objections, but asked the Snake, "Are you sure this is how one gets to be King in this land?" "Plenty sure, Majesty."

9 And so the Snake brought the Mud Doctor, who performed the ceremony making the King a warrior, taking Him deep into the mysteries of the gun.

10 Sacred Mama Love died in Mud City of a broken heart. Though the King rushed to her side, He was too late to save her, and her passing painted a cloud forever over His eyes. Broken by the weight of His grief, He fled her grave to serve the crusade in the Old Lands.

9 *"the Mud Doctor"—Walter Alden, who inducted Elvis into the U.S. Army on March 24, 1958.*

10 *"Sacred Mama Love died…" —Gladys Love Presley, who hadn't wanted Elvis to go into the army, died on August 14, 1958, in Memphis.*

THE VIRGIN

1 After the death of Sacred Mama Love, the King became like an empty man. Defending with His brother soldiers the borders of the New Land of a Thousand Years, He would stare out over the frozen land to the dreaded Sharing Empire beyond. He began experimenting with potions to conquer the sloth. Some said He spent His time off guard taking a soldier's commonest pay in the cup and in the bed, and He did little to quiet the

1 *"potions to conquer the sloth"* —*amphetamines.*

rumors, but in truth He spent the nights weeping for the arms of Sacred Mama Love, forever lost to Him. He became a wilderness like unto the cold steppe of the Old Lands where He wandered.

2 Then, at an officer's house in one of the garrison towns, He had His first vision of the Virgin. She was young and new as the spring, pure as the love of Sacred Mama Love, a vision in blue and white. Within the space of a heartbeat, the King was under her spell and had pledged her His love.

3 Aware of His love and desire, she teased Him unmercifully, as young girls will. Still, she felt His love was a pure one, springing like a seedling from the

2 *"the Virgin"*—
Priscilla Ann Beaulieu. "vision in blue and white"— Priscilla's dress when they first met.

buried flower of the love of His Sacred Mama, and she pledged her love for Him in return.

4 The Virgin was a young girl, not a free woman, and was in the care of a commander in the army, so the King could not claim her while He was a soldier. Instead He was made to court her and win her like a stammering boy half His age.

5 And so He did, and so He would, for years to come.

4 *"a commander in the army"*— *Priscilla's stepfather Joseph Beaulieu was actually a captain in the U.S. Air Force.*

THE CONTEST WITH FAUST

1 When the King had served His term in the army of Plenty, He was held up to the fathers of Beaver by none other than Faust, surrounded by the Bishop, the Kid, and the Moor. Faust was known to have the most powerful spells over women in all of Plenty and he playfully challenged the King to a competition of power. The King demurred, but Faust pressed Him, saying, "Surely you don't claim to match my

1 The story of "The Frank Sinatra-Timex Special," an ABC show taped in Miami on March 26, 1959, with Sinatra, Joey Bishop ("the Bishop"), Nancy Sinatra ("the Kid"), and Sammy Davis, Jr. ("the Moor"). The "spells," as well as signifying the power Sinatra and Elvis had over women, also refers to Elvis's selection of

Sinatra's hit "That Old Black Magic" when Sinatra did "Hound Dog." Elvis's duet with Nancy was, co-incidentally, her hit "Witch-craft."

2 "the Sphinx"— orchestra leader Nelson Riddle.

3 "the Prince of Lies"—the Devil.

magic, Little Majesty? Let me show you how it's done."

2 And he called to the Sphinx who caused the musicians to play the theme of one of the King's spells, but Faust began chanting in a mocking, singsong voice. The women at the gathering began to shout and laugh.

3 The King was angered at Faust's mockery, and began chanting one of Faust's spells. The women began to cry and moan. Soon the King had turned the women of the gathering to His converts, for none could resist the spell of the King's voice. Smiling, Faust conceded the contest. Privately, he made a note to speak with the Prince of Lies.

4 After the contest with Faust, no one in Plenty challenged the King again. The fathers of Beaver could not deny His kingdom, for He had joined their most holy worship of War. He was proclaimed King of all the lands of Plenty and beyond. Faust himself had given his daughter to greet the King when He returned from the army, and later gave his concubine to play beside the King in a shadow-picture.

5 No one questioned the King about what He did with Faust's women, nor with any other. Nor did any dare ask Him of his pledge to the Virgin, not even the Snake, who never waited to bait the King.

4 *Faust's daughter —Nancy Sinatra. Faust's concubine —uncertain. Natalie Wood has been suggested as the identity of the "concubine," but although she and Elvis dated in 1956, they never made a film together.*

6 For the King kept His pledge in His soul, and no other woman but the Virgin meant anything to Him. Still, He took the spoils due a King of Plenty, urged on by the Snake, who was, as promised, a man of the World. The King began to be torn in two, between the purity of His love for the Virgin and the wantonness of His deeds.

THE CROSS OF LIGHT

1 All of Plenty was Shaking, and with it Shook the World. The wizards and craftsmen of Plenty brought forth earthly miracles, from radios no bigger than a man's hand to fantastic ships sailing to the far side of the earth with gift baskets of hellfire. The worship of War was made mandatory, with the crusade now marking a line around the whole World. The endless, ritual spirit-war against the Sharers had not cooled below blood

See Matthew 4, Mark 1:2, Luke 4.

1 "gift baskets of hellfire"—nuclear weapons. "spirit-war"—cold war. "YellowMan's Land"—Asia. "A man... leaving the world itself"—Alan Shepard's space flight. "One million men and women..."—Freedom Riders and other civil rights activists.

temperature in the YellowMan's Land since before the reign of Great War the Son. One man of Plenty became known by leaving the World itself, and coming back alive. One million men and women of Plenty became known by proclaiming themselves men and women. It was the Year Everything Turned Upside Down.

2 When the Upside-Down Year had come, the King received a messenger from Mephistopheles in Babylon. The Old One sent greetings and salutations and begged the King's presence in his glowing capital in the golden desert. The King asked the Snake the meaning of the invitation, but the Snake professed to know nothing.

2 *"Upside-Down Year"—1961. Refers not only to the revolutionary nature of the year, but the fact that the number reads the same upside-down. "Mephistopheles"—the Devil.*

3 When the King's party arrived at the city gates, the multitudes came out to see and hear Him. Everywhere was light and spectacle. The arenas boasted the brightest shows, the games of chance whispered of gold without work, maidens were laid out like courses in a feast. The King loved it all.

4 Mephistopheles was the perfect host to the King, taking Him to every gambling den and counting house, every theater and brothel, even securing Him a golden afternoon with Lapin, the legendary hetaera of Babylon.

4 *"Lapin"*— *Ann-Margret, the toast of Las Vegas, was known by the code names Bunny and Thumper (the rabbit from the Disney film* Bambi) *when visiting Elvis.*

5 After several days and nights of debauchery, Mephistopheles and the King climbed the walls of the Old One's

palace and looked out over the gaudy city, its famed streets of light like a great cross challenging the desert stars.

6 "This is the World, Majesty. Not the cities of Empire and Heaven, nor even the city of Marble where the fathers of Beaver cut the earth in two to worship Almighty War. Here in this nest of lights is the capital of the dark heart of man. Here every man thinks he can be king, and no one deceives himself about the price to be paid. Have you the strength to rule such a tribe, Majesty? Are you truly King of kings, or merely a king of Beavers?"

7 "What do you want of me?" asked the King.

8 "Only that you should make Babylon your capital, your Majesty. From here you may survey all the lands of Plenty and beyond. From every corner the princes of the World come here to worship the cross of light with gold and human sacrifice. Ruling here, from its center, you can build an empire that will endure a thousand years. You will have powers beyond the wizards, greater than the greatest Voices. You will be as a god."

9 "What do you want of me?" the King asked again.

10 "His Majesty knows the price," replied the Old One, looking out over the cross of light.

8 *"the cross of light"—the famed Las Vegas Strip.*

11 "And the Snake?" asked the King.

12 The Old One laughed. "The Snake shall always take his share, Majesty, and shall share the cost as well."

13 The King looked down upon the cross and prayed, but no vision came to Him, neither of the Virgin nor His Sacred Mama Love, only the endless river of worshippers at the cross. And the King knew that Mephistopheles had spoken the truth, that the fathers of Beaver and the boyars of the Sharing Empire and all the princes and princesses of the World would acknowledge only one King: He Who Won. The best of them were thieves and harlots, and they were kings because they at least were honest.

14 Then said the King: "Get thee behind me, and push."

15 So the King set His seal upon the cross of light, and the Old One proclaimed Him Exalted of Babylon, emperor of the World.

THE SAVIOR

1 For the next two years, the King seemed little changed by His elevation in Babylon. He still spent much time at the residence in Mud City, where He had built a shrine to the Virgin, which she consecrated, but traveled often to the city of Heaven to make shadow-pictures, or to Babylon to consult with the Old One or visit with Lapin. The King even brought the craftsmen of Babylon to make a shadow-picture of Himself and

1 Long Live
Babylon—
The film Viva
Las Vegas
*starring Elvis
and Ann-Mar-
gret.*

Lapin, which was called *Long Live Babylon*.

2 Still, the King summoned the Virgin to the residence, where she lived openly as His consort and, most assumed, His concubine as well. Aided by the powers of the Old One and the spells of the Snake, no one spoke against Him. By their laws, the fathers of Beaver could have persecuted the King. The fathers had tried the Duck for just the same crime. Instead, the fathers voted to bestow upon the King a new title: lucky so-and-so. The King accepted graciously.

3 The fathers of Beaver had mellowed. They had chosen a new leader, Savior. Though a war hero like the Bald

One, he was a young man with the power to dream. Many have since said that Savior was truly the King of Plenty and that the King was the Antiking. Surely Savior had the King's power to capture the spirits of women, but the fathers of Beaver approved of him because he had driven the hellfire engines of the Sharers from the Tiny Island off the coast of Plenty. Therefore, the fathers ate not of the sour grapes, but proclaimed Savior a lucky so-and-so.

4 Like all rulers of Plenty since before the times of Grandfather War, Savior had made an oath to World, that he would do the will of World in all

"hellfire engines...Tiny Island"— the Cuban Missile Crisis. "the fathers ate not of the sour grapes..." See Ezekiel 18:2.

4 *"Grandfather War"—American Civil War.*

things, and that Plenty should be unto the world a picture of the World to be.

5 But World trusted not the oath of Savior, and feared that Savior meant to fulfill the prophecies of the deists who had founded Plenty: the kingdom of Self. This was not the will of World, so World set traps for Savior, offering thirty pieces of silver to any and all takers.

6 Then entered World into Judas, surnamed Isecretagent, being of the number of the alone. And he went his way, and Savior was duly crucified.

7 After three days the hangar door was rolled open and out stepped Savior's man Rodeo Clown who carried on in Savior's name.

5 "deists"—U.S. Founding Fathers

6 "Judas...Isecretagent, being of the number of the alone"—Lee Harvey Oswald, one of a number of alleged political assassins described as "lone madmen."

7 "Rodeo Clown"—Lyndon B. Johnson.

8 Though He felt the sorrow of Plenty and all the people of the world at the crucifixion of Savior, the King felt there was little He could do to help either Rodeo Clown or Savior's poor widow. He sent His sorrows and His blessings to both and got back to making plans to do battle with the invading Dukes of the Olde Worlde. Presently, ministers from the city of Marble came secretly to the King's residence and asked the King to take the leadership of Plenty from Rodeo Clown.

9 "I am King of Plenty and all the lands beyond," the King told them. "I am emperor of the World, proclaimed in Babylon. There has never been another

8 *"Savior's poor widow"* — Jacqueline Kennedy Onassis. *"Dukes of the Olde Worlde"* — The Beatles. *"ministers... take the leadership of Plenty"* — There is a story that Elvis was asked, seriously, to run for president after JFK's assassination.

king with so many gold tablets to proclaim his power. Let the fathers of Beaver
choose the Clown or another to lead
Plenty. The World is my empire!"

10 The ministers left the residence
humbled, but for His part the King slept
badly that night, seeing Savior's face
before Him.

The Conquerors from the Olde Worlde

1 Around the time of Savior's crucifixion, there came across the sea from the Olde Worlde voices like unto the Voices Beaver first heard upon the Radio, some said like unto the voice of the King Himself. It was said that chiefs of these voices, called the Dukes, had dethroned the King in the Olde Worlde and even in the New Land of a Thousand Years.

2 Soon the Dukes arrived in Plenty and a procession was held in the city of

1 *"Olde Worlde"—England.*

Empire. When the Dukes were brought before the gathering of the Big Showman, the Snake hastily sent a message in the King's Name welcoming the Dukes to Plenty and offering them His protection and blessing. "Why would you do that?" asked the King. The Snake answered: "If you do not publicly welcome the Dukes, they will think you fear them, that you believe they mean to conquer you." "And so they do!" cried the King. "But they cannot, unless you allow them to. If you acknowledge their power, they will have conquered without a fight. By offering your protection, you claim them as your lieges, as dukes should be to a king."

3 So in the Stuttering Year, the King granted the Dukes of the Olde Worlde an audience, and the Dukes came and gave homage and sang the praises of the King. Still, like Faust, the Dukes could not resist teasing the King. One of them, St. Francis the Sissy, offered to make the King one of them.

4 "Ah, but that would not be fair," said the King, "for could the four of you become one of me?"

3 *"the Stuttering Year"*— 1965, the year The Who released "My Generation": "St. Francis the Sissy"—John Lennon.

THE SHAKING WITHIN

1 Still, the King worried about the Dukes, and the Woodsman and the wizard from the West called Sailor. He went to the Snake and voiced His fears: "Reptile, while I turn out these idiot parable shadow-pictures year by year, wizards and warriors from all lands are finding new spells and powers unknown to me. Why, it has been more than a handful of years since I Shook at a gathering."

1 *"the Woodsman" —Bob Dylan, from the north woods of Minnesota. "Sailor"—the Beach Boys' Brian Wilson, from his song "Sail On, Sailor."*

2 The Snake spoke quickly: "Majesty, these shouters and writhers cannot touch you. They are not even the shadows of the Voices of old, let alone your regal self. Their spells are merely tricks, but you have the power to Shake, to Cry, to Die. You have the King's voice and the crown of the World. What need have you to prance before some gathering of common drunkards and fools? And those shadow-pictures you speak of, are they not beloved by the multitudes?" The Snake continued until the King had been soothed or distracted. Not once did the Scaled One speak of the millionbuck of gold he and the King shared for every shadow-picture.

3 But the King had not been mistaken. Wizards, princes and pretenders everywhere began calling upon a new power: the Shaking within. The King did not understand their words. At times they seemed to speak of the mystery teachings of the Yellow Man's Land, then without stopping they would be talking of radios and microphones. It all seemed to have something to do with a particular potion.

4 Among the King's court was a coiffeur named Starman, who had been schooled in various mysteries of the eastern lands. He initiated the King into the mysteries of the Yellow Man, and it was said that in those days the King discov-

3 *"the Shaking within"—the psychedelic experience.*

4 *"Starman"— Elvis's hairdresser and spiritual adviser Larry Geller. May also refer to the Star Man, a Polish Father Christmas figure, emphasizing Geller's "gift" of spiritual instruction.*

"the secret potion of the shaking within"—LSD.
"the potion of wakefulness"—amphetamines.
"the potion of sleep"—barbiturates.

ered the secret potion of Shaking within, but the King preferred the potion of wakefulness He had discovered in the army of Plenty, and the potion of sleep which countered it.

THE YEAR OF THE LONG HAIR

1 The year following Sailor's dissertation on the Shaking within, the King took the Virgin to Babylon and there in the presence of World and the Old One made her His legal wife. The King was happier than He could remember, but He was beginning to remember less and less as He grew more sickened from potions.

2 But something else happened that year which shook the King and all the lands of the world, shook World itself as

1 *"Sailor's dissertation"—The Beach Boys' "Good Vibrations."*

2 *"Sir George"—The Beatles' producer George Martin. "City of the Gate"—San Francisco, referring both to the Golden Gate Bridge and San Francisco's reputation as the gateway to the psychedelic hippie life. "The Voice-picture"—"Sgt. Pepper's Lonely Hearts Club Band." "Doughboy"—Rolling Stone editor Jan Wenner. "the Glass-Eyed Ghost"—Phil Spector.*

much as had the King at the Shrine of St. Luke. Across the sea, the Dukes and their specter Sir George had been studying the dissertation of the Sailor and the obscure spells of the tribes of the City of the Gate in Plenty. The Dukes would swallow the secret potion and chant while Sir George wove spells with the microphone that had never been made before. When the voice-pictures of their ritual were sent out to all the lands, many claimed the voice-pictures themselves were not frozen, but alive with the Shaking within. It was proclaimed throughout all the lands that the Dukes' ritual would thereafter be known as The Voice-picture. "There is no other!" cried the prophet Doughboy, and no one, not Sailor, nor the Glass-Eyed Ghost nor the King Himself, could gainsay it. So it has been called unto this day.

3 The Voice-picture lit a fire among the young of every land. In Plenty, sons and daughters of the fathers of Beaver who had never heard of the Shaking within, some who barely knew of Shaking without, cried for a taste of the secret potion. Countless multitudes made pilgrimages across Plenty to the City of the Gate, there to grow their hair and forget the teachings of their fathers. The prophets called it the Year of the Long Hair, and prophesied the fall of World.

3 *"the Year of the Long Hair"*—1967.

THE YEAR OF THE REVOLUTION

1 The year following the Year of the Long Hair, all the prophecies of the fall of World seemed closer and farther than ever to becoming real. World showed his might, and felled the Healer of the hot, dark people in Mud City, then Fulton, the brother of Savior in the city of Heaven. For a time it was feared that the Sharers would overwhelm the forces of Plenty in the YellowMan's Land.

1 *"the Healer"*— Rev. Dr. Martin Luther King, Jr. "Fulton"—Robert F. Kennedy, the assumed derivation being from the Old English fula-tun, *or "the people's estate." "it was feared that the Sharers..."*— the Tet offensive in Vietnam.

2 *"Happy"—Hubert H. Humphrey. "the Crossburner"—George Wallace. "Rubber Man"—Richard M. Nixon.*

2 Rodeo Clown abdicated the throne of Plenty and left his man Happy to fight with the Crossburner and Rubber Man for it. The youth of Plenty had overtaken the *lycea* and *collegia* and sex became something spoken of in the light of day on the public way. Nothing was what it had been, nothing would be as it was.

3 *"Year of the Revolution"—1968. "Little Virgin"— Lisa Marie Presley, born February 1, 1968.*

3 Throughout this Year of the Revolution, the King brooded. Though the Virgin had brought forth a child, Little Virgin, He felt lost and confused. He had no idea of where He fit in a world turned around. The potions he swallowed had robbed much of His power, and World waited for Him to die the true death.

4 Then, at the Feast of the Child, the King called a gathering on the picture-radio, to be held throughout the land of Plenty. Great were the expectations of the people of Plenty, for none had seen the King but in shadow-pictures for almost a half score years. As the preparations were being made for the gathering, the King walked alone the streets of the city of Heaven, and the people knew Him not.

5 The feast season began and the King went before the multitudes and reviewed His life; He called forth the Voices of the Shrines of Father Sam and St. Luke, and harkened back to the days when they would Die together; He sent

4 *"Feast of the Child"—Christmas. The NBC "comeback" special on December 3, 1968, with Scotty Moore, D.J. Fontana and Charlie Hodge.*

5 *"His dream"—Elvis performed the song "If I Can Dream" on the broadcast.*

forth the King's voice, telling of His dream.

6 And the multitudes of Plenty were awed and ashamed, and they sent their voices unto the King, crying, "Forgive us, Once and Future King, for we had forgotten thy glory. Be thou ever our king, and we shall not forget thee again."

7 "Then follow me to Babylon," commanded the King, "and the gathering shall never end!"

BABYLON

1 In Babylon, the King renounced the kings of the shadow-pictures in the city of Heaven and called for a Gathering without End and a Procession to Everywhere. The court dressed Him in His royal vestments of the whitest hart skin, adorned with precious metals and gems. Without the gold from the shadow-pictures, the Snake began charging the mayors of Babylon a halfmillionbuck of gold for every moon cycle the gathering went on.

1 *"...renounced the kings of shadow-picture... Procession to Everywhere"—except for the documentaries "Elvis—That's the Way It Is" and "Elvis on Tour," Elvis made no films after 1969, but concentrated on his Vegas appearances and extended touring. "halfmillionbuck of gold... moon cycle"—Actually, the contract, signed by Parker*

on a tablecloth, called for Elvis to be paid $1 million per year, but Elvis performed only two months out of the year.

2 World summoned the Snake and told him: "You have stolen more than enough half-kingdoms, Scaled One, but still you want more. You cannot seem to make yourself bring the King to true death, nor with potions nor the killing chariot nor the sacred gun. Do you dream of forever sucking half the teats of this golden cow, or will you perform your pledge and kill Him?"

3 The Snake replied that he could not kill the King. "Lord, all could see at the gathering at the Feast of the Child, He cannot die the true death. He has Died and will choose the time of His dying."

4 World grew angry, and shouted at the Snake, "Who art thou to tell me what

4 See Job 38, 39. "the Mole"—James Earl Ray,

cannot be done? Hast thou seen through the eye of the Mole, or the Zealot, or the loneliest demonmad Judas Isecretagent? Hast thou crucified the Lizard, or drowned the Lady? Hast thou like me choked the life from the Gypsy with the word of his own bliss? Thou canst not kill the King, Snake, but thou art not the whole World, thou knowest."

5 Rumors reached the court that assassins hunted the King, and all the King's men were trained in the fighting ways of the YellowMan's Land, and each pledged to the sacred gun. They vowed that He would not be another Savior.

6 The King Himself balanced potions and spells, gazed upon crystals

presumably referring to his brief escape from prison in 1977. "the Zealot"— Sirhan Sirhan. "the Lizard" —Jim Morrison, known as the Lizard King. "the Lady"— Janis Joplin. "the Gypsy"— Jimi Hendrix.

5 "fighting ways of the Yellow-Man's Land"—Elvis was a black belt in karate and required his bodyguards to train in the martial arts.

and candles, lived in a world between the world and World, and knew the mysteries of all places and things. Still He Shook at the Gathering without End and along the Procession to Everywhere, though He was no more there than He was everywhere and it sometimes appeared that the King was no longer Shaking the people, but that they were Shaking for Him.

7 Then one night, awash in a sea of potions He could not remember taking, a vision opened before the King of the time at the beginning of Time.

THE KING'S VISION: THE ARMIES OF OTHERMIND

1 In the beginning of all Time when God commanded man to make world of Earth, he made for man the force of Othermind to grow bricks to make world.

2 So great was the force of Othermind that God feared man would seek it only and never would he be in his right mind, wherefore did God split the Othermind into two: Ol, the goddess of sleep, to draw man down into dark slumber and forgetfulness, and Ine, the god of

1 *"make world of Earth"*—Refers to the abstracting (modeling) of the world in the mind, hallmark of modern human "consciousness." See J. Jaynes, The Origins of Consciousness in the Breakdown of the Bicameral Mind. *See also Genesis 3 and the strange fragment in J. Robinson, ed., "The Gospel of Phillip,"* in Nag Hammadi Library in

English ("*Now the existence of world depends on man...* ").

2 "*Othermind*"— *alternative consciousness. See A. Weil,* The Natural Mind. "*split the Othermind into two,*" *similar to Lao Tzu's Taoist creation story of the universe splitting into the first duality, yin and yang. See A. Waley,* Three Ways of Thought in Ancient China.

wakefulness, to excite man into light and action. Forever pulled between the forces of Ol and Ine, man might have a mind to make a world.

3 Ol and Ine made unto themselves flesh on Earth to pull on the mind of man. The first incarnation of Ol was Alcohol the Inexorable and many were her generations. Out of Alcohol was brought forth Phenobarbitol, and Phenobarbitol begat Seconal, and Seconal begat Tuinal, and Tuinal begat the brothers Demerol and Nembutal, who begat Dilaudid, Quaalude and the twin warriors Elavil and Maravil. Of the line of Thorazine came Librax, Lithium, Librium, Valium, the mighty Xanax and

Prozac the Younger. Of Opium, sister of Alcohol, came the little sister Morphine, who begat Heroin, called the Monkey, mother of Methadone the Impostor, and Codeine the Schoolboy, and Codeine begat Paregoric and Tylenol the Third.

4 The first incarnations of Ine were Ephedrine the Omnipresent, and Ephedrine's younger brother Caffeine, and Ephedrine begat Benzedrine, and Benzedrine begat Dexedrine, and Dexedrine begat Methedrine, and out of Methedrine was brought forth Ice the Terrible, as from Cocaine the Enchantress was brought Crack the Enslaver.

5 *"leaves to cover his nakedness"—marijuana. See Genesis 3:7; "manna"——psychedelics. "rained from the earth"—psylocybin mushrooms. "in the glory of the morning"—lysergic acid, the chemical basis of LSD-25, found in ergot of rye and the seeds of morning glory flowers.*

5 Caught between the armies of Ol and Ine, man was afraid, and cried out. And Earth heard man's cry and sent leaves to cover his nakedness, and manna that would be rained from the Earth and burst forth in the glory of the morning, so that man might have an Othermind of his own beyond the kingdoms of Ol and Ine and build a world of more than either and or.

THE BANISHMENT

1 Before He could remember or interpret it, the King's vision splintered like the forces of Othermind, each fragment sundering again and again, until little remained but empty pictures He could not separate from World's images of gathering and procession.

2 For a time out of Time the King floated in a sea of endlessly mirrored visions. Most of them He forgot, but one made a home in His heart: a picture of the

2-4 *Elvis dismissed Parker in 1973, then began an exceptionally wild period that ended with his teenage companion overdosing on cough syrup. Elvis's aide Joe Esposito ("Teller" from the Latin ex-ponere: to set forth, explain) recalled Parker, who hushed up the incident.*

Snake cutting Him in half over and over and Himself becoming smaller and smaller. The King ordered the Snake banished.

3 With the Snake gone from Babylon, the King ran wild like a man beset by demons. He took more and more potions, and He would take to the streets in His chariot, gathering up maidens from the streets of Babylon. The men of the King's court labored mightily to keep word of His rampages from the people of Plenty and from the Virgin, and they feared for the life of the King.

4 Then one night, the King's man Teller sent a message to the Snake that he must return, for the King had nearly

killed a maiden with too many potions,
trying to find again the vision of
Othermind.

GOLGOTHA

1 The Snake returned to Babylon and took the King to the palace of the Old One. "So, Son of Love, the time comes when all debts must be paid."

2 And the King, hearing the Old One speak of His Sacred Mama, knew that He had sinned against her when He had taken the vow of the gun, and when He had let the Old One crown him emperor in Babylon, and when He had forsaken the sacred powers of Shaking and

Crying and Dying for the vision of the Othermind. He knew His sin and His debt, and climbed the cross of light in the heart of Babylon to await the true death.

3 And the people of Plenty cried out "Terrible, terrible!" and laid upon Him the weight of their own sins and debts.

4 The Snake, for his half, proclaimed the crucifixion to be part of the Gathering without End, and kept bringing in the millionbucks. The Old One rendered unto World what was World's and the spectacle was made into a picture-radio simulgathering in Paradise, the first gathering ever to be held in all lands of the World at once. At the simul-

4 *"the simulgathering in Paradise"—"Elvis: Aloha from Hawaii" was broadcast January 14, 1973 to a worldwide audience of one billion. One of the first global simulcasts. "the way"—Elvis sang "My Way" in the broadcast. "blessed the women... gambled for his robes"—reference to Elvis's*

gathering the King taught of the way, and blessed the women of the world with His raiment, and soon all the peoples of every land gambled for His robes.

5 The Virgin came to the King on the cross, begging Him to come down and live again with her in the residence. The King kissed her and blessed her, then banished her, saying, "This I must do, that thou mayest live." Lapin was allowed to remain with the King, and she faithfully attended Him, sitting daily at the foot of the cross.

6 For two years, from the beheading of Rubber Man to the elevation of James the Good to the throne of Plenty, the King hung on the cross of light. He

scarves, passed to women at concerts and now valuable collectibles.

5 *"The Virgin… banished her"—Priscilla filed for divorce in August of 1972. The action was finalized on October 11, 1973.*

6 *"the beheading of Rubber Man"—resignation of Richard Nixon in 1974. "James the Good"—Jimmy Carter.*

"Fingers"—Ginger Alden, Elvis's last girlfriend and daughter of Capt. Joseph Alden, the officer who inducted Elvis into the army. See "The Warrior King 9."

7 *"Arimathean"—Joseph of Aramathea, who took Christ's body from the cross. See Matthew 27:57-60, Mark 15:43-46, Luke 23:50-53, John 19:38-40. "dragged the king's chariot"—reference to the tour of Elvis's gold Cadillac promoted by Parker in 1966.*

called to Sacred Mama Love, "Why have you forsaken me?" He pointed to Fingers, the daughter of the Mud Doctor who had initiated Him into the spirit-war. "There is my Mother!" He called to the Snake, saying, "You were my only friend." And then He died.

7 The Snake, who might have been Arimathean to the King, was too busy collecting rent on the cross to notice that the King had died. The procession rolled onward, the Snake in the van, parading the King's body through Plenty, as once had the reptile dragged the King's chariot. World finally had the King for a golem, using His own potions and spells to keep the body fresh and the multitudes

to Shake it as once He Shook them. World reached out his hand and worked the King's mouth, making a squeaking mockery of the King's voice raving "Glory, Glory" dripping corpse sweat. The Snake applauded, saying He looked better than He had in years. The gathering continued and the procession proceeded.

"Glory, Glory" reference to Elvis's "Dixie"/"Battle Hymn of the Republic" medley

APOCOPE NOW

1 Green King asked the Snake to leave the body at the residence between gatherings along the procession and the Snake was happy to oblige. The debts postponed by the spells and potions grew overdue, and His Majesty was in truth starting to get a little ripe.

2 The daughter of the Mud Doctor, Fingers, complained to Green King of the smell and he summoned World's Greek physician, who pronounced Him

(From the Greek apokope: the loss of one or more sounds or letters at the end of a word. Reference to the addition of an "A" to the beginning of Elvis's middle name on his grave marker at Graceland. Given the details of Elvis's life and death that the author covers in the Gospel, it is doubtful that this reversal is inadvertent. It has been sug-

gested that the author may be mocking the "Elvis-is-alive" conspiracy theorists who interpret the misspelling as proof of Elvis's survival. Most likely, though, the insertion is changed to deletion to underline the fact that Parker continued to take his "half-kingdom" after Elvis's death. See "Acts of the Apostrophes 2."

2 "World's Greek physician"— Dr. George C. Nichopoulos, who signed Elvis's death certificate after Ginger Alden found Elvis dead in his bathroom on August 16, 1977.

dead upon His throne. As the people of Mud City gathered around the residence, the people of Plenty slowly swelling the crowd, none was heard to cry "Long live the King," for all knew there was none who could follow Him. There would be one King, forever.

3 On the third day, the Snake rose from his hole, taking a letter of the King's Name from His tomb and hanging it around his neck. He pulled the Virgin and Green King to his side and spoke the eulogy:

4 "The King has gone to join His Sacred Mama Love in the kingdom beyond. We are robbed of all the light in the world. What shall become of this

young poor widow and the King's child? What of His loyal father, Green King? What shall become of all of us? How shall we keep Him close to our hearts and thoughts?"

5 "Let us all bow to the King's icons, so that He may watch over all of our lives, in our homes and hearths, in our chariots and temples. Let there be no end to the voice-pictures and shadows, the picture-radio gatherings and passion plays. May His Name be held sacred and endure as World endures."

6 The Snake took the Virgin and Green King by the hand. "King was He as He could Die. Now He has died that we may live, and King He ever shall be."

5 *"King's icons"—Elvis souvenirs. "passion plays"— Elvis impersonators.*

THE ACTS OF THE APOSTROPHES

1 In the first year of the reign of Bald One the Second of Plenty, who was known as Rubber Man's Revenge, the judges of Plenty granted a petition in the name of the poor widowed Virgin and Little Virgin, sundering the Snake for all time from the Name of the King. "Thou wast given half a King's feast," they told the Snake. "Now His table is set with dust, and half of that also is thine." The King's followers rejoiced that the widow

1 "Bald One Second... Rubber Man's Revenge"— Ronald Reagan. In 1981, Parker lost much money and most of his influence over Elvis's estate, a process completed in 1983 when Parker sold his rights in Elvis's records to RCA for $2,000,000 and relinquished all rights to the use of Elvis's name.

and her daughter would no longer have to share the King's fortune with the Snake, and it was said that the quality of the icons improved markedly as well.

2 The Snake came before World outside the walls of Babylon to complain, but World heard him not. "The judges have spoken, and the King's prophecy is fulfilled. Reptile, thou hast taken the letter of the Name in vain."

3 "But we had a deal," protested the Snake. "Tell it to the judges," World replied, "and let not the gate hit thy ass on thy way out."

4 "Good-bye, cruel World," said the Snake, and went on his belly to eat the King's dust. He lived on for generations

in Plenty, forever outside the empire of the King and the glory of His Name.

5 The Virgin continued to control the kingdom of the King's Name for many years, until Little Virgin was a woman. Many in Plenty were afraid for Little Virgin, for she had become a follower of the prophet called Space Invader, and the people of Plenty feared the Little Virgin's brain had been washed whiter than the King's whitest vestments.

6 The Virgin spoke to the people, saying: "The King declared Little Virgin heir to all His kingdom and ruler of His Name. Who among you shall come forward and say he is wiser than the King? If Little Virgin should decide the Space

5 *"Space Invader" —science fiction author L. Ron Hubbard, who founded the Church of Scientology. Lisa Marie Presley is a member.*

Invader should have all the King's wealth, even unto His Name, so must it be. Your faith in Him must extend to His faith in Little Virgin." Then the Virgin retired to nun's roles in Heaven's shadow-pictures.

7 So the people of Plenty accepted Little Virgin as the ruler of the King's Name. Some wondered if she would turn over the kingdom to Space Invader, but she never did. Some thought she might have inherited the King's voice, or His powers, but if she had, she revealed it not. "He could really sing," she said. "I only Sang Real." She married another of the Invaded known as Session, and brought forth the grandchildren of the King.

7 *"Sang Real"* —"Royal Blood." Also the "sangraal" or "Holy Grail" of another Elvis. See Baigent, et al., pp. 305-306. "Session"— Lisa Marie's first husband and fellow Scientologist, musician Danny Keough.

8 The men of the King's court dispersed to write the gospels and preserve the memory of the King, or to serve lesser kings in the cities of Heaven and Empire and throughout the world. Some even renounced the King, three times and more, but their stories only added to His greatness and the kingdom of His Name.

8 *"renounced the King, three times and more"*—See Matthew 26:69, Mark 14:66, Luke 22:57, John 18:17.

A ROYAL WEDDING

1 After many years of quiet in the house of the King, whispers were heard that the Little Virgin lived no more as wife to Session, and would take another seed to bind the blood of the King.

2 In the year of Jove's burning, the prophets of the picture-radio spoke of a secret royal wedding between Little Virgin and the Gray King of the city of Wagons, but the people of Plenty would not believe. Then, in the month of Death

2 "the year of Jove's burning"—In July 1994 Comet Shoemaker-Levy 9 struck Jupiter, creating a series of fireballs. "the Gray King"—Michael Jackson. "the city of Wagons"—"Motor City" Detroit, Michigan. "the month of Death by Heat"—August.

by Heat, servants of the King's house went before the people and proclaimed the truth of the prophets: the royal lines were united.

3 Again were the people dismayed with the will of the Little Virgin. "He is no King!" they cried. "He is not even a man, but a golem himself! A despoiler of children! That we have made him a king in the King's absence was the fault of the picture-radio prophets and the Velvet Princess. Let not the Little Virgin suffer for our sins."

4 And again did the Virgin go before the people of Plenty in Little Virgin's support. "Wherefore do you presume to know the mind of the Little

3 *"the Velvet Princess"— Jackson's friend and "National Velvet" star Elizabeth Taylor, who named Jackson "The King of Pop."*

Virgin? The King has bestowed upon her his trust and the treasure of His Name, and she has borne it well. Now she is a woman and it is a woman's call she follows. That her path leads unto the house of Gray is a blessing and a goodness. Blood royal flows ever downward and is lost without a dam to draw its stream back into itself. In the Gray King she shall be as a right and proper dam and I don't give one."

4 *"dam"— used as "mother" and as a dam to conserve royal blood.*

5 Still did the people of Plenty wail at the union, for they did not know the mysteries of She Who Sang Real, but the Little Virgin heard them not, and pledged herself unto the Gray King, and thus were joined the greatest houses of

Plenty, that the King's blood and the King's Name might endure the ages.

6 So is written the chronicle of the King and those He left behind. Now have His Name and graven image spread to all the lands of the World and none shall have the excuse of ignorance when called to acknowledge Him. Even the moving stars above shall bow to the time of His passing, and His Name shall be a treasure forever.

SOLOMON'S FIRST LETTER TO THE PLENTIANS

1 Greetings to you in the Name of the King. Blessings and praise unto the people of Plenty in the Name of the King.

2 There is but one Plenty, alone among lands founded on the power of the kingdom of Self. Even in the darkness of the last days are her children blessed, and the King could not have sprung from any other land.

3 Children of Plenty, this you must not forget: You are the people who have

given the King to this world and to this World. For who among you has not denied Him, yet who among you has not made himself but an icon of the King?

4 There is but one king. Though the learned monks speak now of kings, when they ought speak of Voices or study their stars, the Name of the King is never mistaken for the name of a man.

5 Despair not of the mummers and Lousirs who take His Name in vain, for they only praise Him in the sincerest form. Never is it heard, "He is the King," but merely, "Is he not as unto the King in a small way?" The kings of small ways and pretenders without end shall not know the glory of His Name.

5 *"mummers"— Elvis impersonators. "Lousir"— Elvis Costello, after Lou Costello, and the author's designation of British men as "sir" (see "The Year of the Long Hair").*

6 There is but one King as there is one World shaped by War the Son, one generation of Beavers in a Plenty that shall never be again. But so long as the sons and daughters of Beaver have sons and daughters, they shall have no other king before Him, unto the last days.

7 I tell you in that time, they will say to you, "He is there, in the market" or "He is there, where they beat the clothes by the river," and they shall be amazed that He lives.

8 Be ye not amazed then, for what has made Him King but that he could Die and live again that His Name might live forever? This news only shall ye believe: He is there, in your heart when

7 *"in the market... beat the clothes by the river"*—Elvis *has been sighted many times since his death, including in a supermarket and in a laundromat. See Matthew 24:23-26, Mark 13:21-23.*

you feel the call to Shake and Cry and dance and Die.

9 Peace be unto you, and unto your children.

COMMENTARY ON THE GOSPEL OF ELVIS

A.L. LUDWIG

AUTHORSHIP AND INTENT OF THE GOSPEL OF ELVIS

Two great questions surround *The Gospel of Elvis*, neither of which is easily answered: Who wrote this, and why?

The question of authorship, seemingly the simpler of the two, proves on examination to be as much of a puzzle as the book's intent. Solomon B.T. Church, the author of record, though accepted by most scholars as a pseudonym, holds some clues. The name, suggesting both Jewish and Catholic traditions, almost certainly derives from the spurious "wash-'n-wear mystery cult" known as Sol's Big and Tall Men's Church—As Seen on TV. The church, according to its literature, has been in existence since 1963, though the oldest documents available for study date from the early 1990s, suggesting that the church is in truth much younger.

Most likely, Sol's is one of the do-it-yourself churches inspired in the late 1980s and early 1990s by the Dallas-based Church of the SubGenius Foundation. Other examples of these "religions de jure" include ICHOP—The International Church of Pancakes in Cambridge, Massachusetts, and The Church of Limited Liability, founded by New Orleans attorney Mark J. Davis.

That S.B.T. Church can be proved a pseudonym tells us little about the person or persons behind it, other than the already known fact that they are not lacking in a sense of humor about religious matters. Izquierdo cites differences in narrative style throughout

≈

the *Gospel*—differences which cannot be explained by the effects of multiple translations—as proof that the book is not the work of one person, but a collection of fragments written at different times by many authors. This theory gains credibility when one compares the concrete, almost pedantic style of the King's early years with lyrical and visionary fragments such as "The Armies of Othermind."

Further compounding the problem of attribution is the fact that, like the gospels of Jesus, *The Gospel of Elvis* shows considerable evidence of careful editing and invention to please various power groups. Just as Rome was exonerated in the crucifixion of Jesus by the story of Pilate's hand-washing, obvious concessions have been made by the *Gospel's* authors to the "fathers of Beaver" in the way certain unpleasant truths have been glossed over. The treatment of race relations in particular is notably simplistic, though, it must be added, not dishonestly so.

The task of determining with certainty the authorship of *The Gospel of Elvis* will probably prove impossible. Are we then doomed to remain equally ignorant of its *raison d'être*, or is there a way to decipher the authors' intent from the book itself?

BUILDING THE LANGUAGE OF ELVIS

The Gospel of Elvis is not a simple document. History, theology, humor and allegory intermingle within its pages, sometimes reinforcing one another, sometimes negating one another. Comments from early reviewers range from "Crazy. Funny as hell, but crazy," to "a peek at the world's next major religion."

That latter statement brings to the forefront the crucial question in any discussion of the *Gospel*: Is this for real? Elvis the god?

The *Gospel* is not the first document to treat Elvis as a religious figure. There are three known churches of Elvis and countless buttons, stickers, graffiti and T-shirts proclaiming the King's divinity. In his 1991 book, *Dead Elvis*, Greil Marcus offers some useful context on this Elvis worship. It is Marcus's theory that, since August 16, 1977, when the King died holding a book about the shroud of Turin, the entire world has joined in the task of his resurrection. By constantly manipulating and rebroadcasting the millions of images, sounds, and ideas associated with Elvis Presley, we are weaving him so tightly into the collective unconscious that he will never truly die.

There is a price for this immortality, however: Elvis's reality as a human being, a man who was born in a particular place, had a lifetime of experiences and then, as we all must, came to ground. But any "real" life, even one as exciting and unique as Elvis's, is too limited to contain the vast mythological figure he was destined to become. His death was only one step in shedding that humanity, not the first step by many.

In *Lives of a Cell*, Lewis Thomas posits that humans, like the social insects, follow the instinctual pattern of hive-building, each individual hauling and placing the materials for a structure larger than any individual, or generation, can build. Our hives, claims Thomas, are not our cities but our languages, where we truly live. If Marcus is right, and Elvis Presley is becoming a language, some of its volumes must surely be religious works. [1]

For the sake of argument, we shall assume that the *Gospel* is meant, at least in part, as a book of religious instruction. What sort of religion is it meant to teach? To simply respond, "Why, the religion of Elvis, of course," ignores the evolutionary nature of faith. No worship exists in a vacuum, and just as Christianity grew from the foundation of Judaism, which itself refined and reformed earlier Canaanite beliefs, so this "Elvisism" must have its own family tree.

A SACRED SMORGASBORD

That the main branch of this tree should be a Christianity based on strict, literal interpretation of the Holy Bible, King James Version, is obvious. This was the religion of Elvis himself, a young man who dreamed of growing up to be a gospel singing star. It is the religion of the culture that created the man, then made him an immortal king. One cannot possibly understand the King of Western Bop without acknowledging the King to whom he bowed.

But fundamentalist Christianity, by itself, is too small a vessel for a mythos the size of Elvis. Just as the story of Jesus had to be rewritten to reach a wider audience than messianic Jews, *The Gospel of Elvis* was written to reach a world bigger than its roots. If Jesus can be transformed from an anointed king and rabbi to a virgin-born, resurrected Son of God to please Greek and Roman readers, it should be no surprise that *The Gospel of Elvis* reaches beyond Christianity for its proofs of its king's importance. In this light, references like the quasi-Taoist vision of Othermind or the Eleusinian and Arthurian echoes in the King's Dying at the Shrine of St. Luke can be seen as efforts to sell Elvis the King in the global religious market.

Religious double entendres are everywhere to be found among the names given to the *Gospel's* characters. Coyote is an easy play on Alan Freed's nickname

Moondog, but the name also conjures up visions of the Plains Indian legends of Coyote the Trickster, who delights in spreading chaos and confusion among men with his practical jokes. Coyote's pranks usually go awry, and he too gets tricked, but gets away to trick again. The story of Freed's Moondog Coronation Ball concert as told in "The Jamboree " could be a typical Coyote tale.

Vernon Presley's appellation of Green King is more than a play on Vernon/vernal. It also suggests the god/king figure central to European spring carnivals, the peasant chosen as temporary king so that, when the crops are planted, he can be slain and his blood and "powers" spread to assure a good yield, as described in Sir J.G. Frazer's *The Golden Bough*.

THE SNAKE: "JUST DOING MY JOB."

Strangest of all perhaps is the *Gospel's* treatment of "Colonel" Tom Parker. At first glance, identification of Parker with a snake seems simply a scornful reference to the Colonel. Yet this work treats Parker more gently than many others, and the *Gospel's* approach to many subjects, from placing Parker in West Virginia in his early years, to the lack of any mention of Vernon Presley's incarceration for forgery in 1937, conforms strictly to Parkerian legends.

In seeking deeper meanings of serpentine imagery in a document so laced with Jewish ideas and puns, it makes sense to look to the third chapter of Genesis. Here the snake makes his appearance on the world's stage and hasn't gone a minute into his first scene before he's caused all manner of trouble. He convinces Eve, the first and perfect woman, to eat the forbidden fruit of the Tree of Knowledge of Good and Evil. She then persuades Adam to disobey his Lord's only direct prohibition and do likewise, and their first, crude exercise of moral judgment results in their descendants being cursed to work for bread and bear children in pain.

The most common assumption about this passage, that the "serpent" represents Satan, is unsupported by the text. In God's punishment for tempting Eve (verse 14), it is made clear that he is decreeing the lot of real snakes, "cursed above all cattle, and above every beast of the field." What are we to make of a Fall not scripted by supernatural Devil, but merely the preventable accident of creatures too smart for their own good? Shouldn't God have foreseen this regrettable outcome?

In truth, the entire Temptation and Fall smell like a setup: the Lord placed Adam in the garden with explicit instructions about the Tree of Knowledge, then, as he slept, crafted Eve and set her in the garden, where he knew his creature the serpent, "more subtle than any beast of the field which the Lord God had made," dwelt. It appears almost as if God had intended the serpent to tempt mankind with the knowledge reserved for gods, that he might remind us that though we are made in his image, we shall still have no other gods before him, including ourselves.

This interpretation of Genesis 3 as an intentional, scripted lesson in humility is supported by Ronald S. Hendel's eye-opening article in the Biblical Archaeology Review collection, *Understanding the Dead Sea Scrolls*. The article, "When the Sons of God Cavorted with the Daughters of Men," is concerned primarily with another story of human hubris, the divine/mortal miscegenation of Genesis 6:1-4, but

Hendel takes care to place the story in a larger context of tests and transgressions which slowly fix humankind's place in relation to the divine: "The Primeval Cycle in Genesis is characterized by a series of mythological transgressions of boundaries... The mixing of gods and mortals in Genesis 6:1-4 is mirrored by the mixing of the divine and human in the Garden of Eden story, in which humans desire to 'be as gods, knowing good and evil,' another cosmic imbalance."[2]

If the snake was appointed by God to teach his first man the vanity of godlike ambitions, and to make the lessons cruelly just, and suffer himself into the bargain, then "Colonel" Tom was the perfect Snake to the first man of rock and roll. Many have used the word "destiny" in discussing the two men's relationship. The *Gospel* offers glimpses of this karmic bond between the two in the King's acceptance of the Snake, despite the courtiers shock at the Snake's insulting tone in "Half a Kingdom," and even more in the King's declaration that the Snake "was my only friend" in "Golgotha."[3] Perhaps the King knew that the Snake had a crucial role to fulfill in the making of his story.

A SACRED HYPERTEXT

A Brother who shakes. A Savior betrayed by Judas Isecretagent, leaving behind a poor widow. A Priest-king dying and rising again, corrupted by a Snake pledged to bring him the true death. Faust. Caesar. War the Father, Son, and Spirit. Saints, kings, zealots and astronomers. The *Gospel* is like an ancient's memory stick or a hypertext course in comparative religion, each name and word-picture opening to a new story or lesson.

Still, the core message of the *Gospel* can't be grasped simply by chasing down every obscure sacred reference, as if one "can't tell the saints without a score-card." Pointing out the biblical passages in "The Savior" or "The Shrine of Father Sam," or recognizing the Talmudic origins of the "shards" of the spirit in "The Coming of the King" doesn't tell us *why* this book was written.

If this is merely a comparison of the historical Elvis and Jesus, as in A.J. Jacobs's farce *The Two Kings: Jesus-Elvis*, why are there so many references that don't correspond to traditional Christian thought? Why are certain devices repeated so often, such as the King's Dying, the idea of the royal blood, the "Sang Real" of the later books and the constant identification of "World" with Rome, from its creation in "the smashing of all the world's sevens" to details like naming Dr. George Nichopoulos "World's Greek physician," recalling the penchant Roman nobles had for Greek therapists over their own countrymen?

ELVIS THE KING

In their controversial 1982 book *Holy Blood, Holy Grail*, Michael Baigent, Richard Leigh, and Henry Lincoln follow similar threads in the Bible, early gnostic texts, and the Dead Sea Scrolls to a startling, nontraditional picture of Jesus. According to their hypothesis, not unlike that put forth by Hugh Schoenfield in *The Passover Plot,* Jesus was not only a bona fide king of Israel, sworn to topple the hated Roman puppet-kings of Judea, but a shaman as well, schooled in the traditional mystery religions of the Middle East.

Once one accepts that it is this Jesus, this priest-king and revolutionary, who is the model for the King in *The Gospel of Elvis*, the comparisons begin to make sense. And it is in this context of spiritual revolution that one finds the key component of any messianic career: the times.

Both Elvis Aron Presley and Yeshua bar Yusef were born into old, provincial cultures under attack from an omnipotent, invading *Überkultur*. In Jesus' case, the fundamentalist Galilean traditions with which he sought to reform all of Judea were in direct conflict with the state religions of the county's Roman occupiers, indeed with the Roman worldview of state supremacy. To messianic Israelites, no state could demand the allegiance due to God.

As for Elvis, he was born in the American South, a country scorned but still eagerly exploited by its wealthier and more sophisticated neighbors and occupiers, and he came to prominence in the time and context of postwar/cold war America, a culture that valued regimentation, conformism and unquestioning service to the all-wise state. These ideas are alien to the essential rural/frontier American culture, alive in the South well into the twentieth century. This Southern frontier mindset, extensively analyzed in W.J. Cash's *The Mind of the South*, can be summed up in the creed: "Get off my property!" To a patriotic Southerner, no state could demand the autonomy due to the individual.

Elvis's career and the careers he inspired were more than the stories of entertainers getting lucky and achieving popularity and success. A careful reading of the *Gospel* suggests that rock and roll was in truth a *jihad,* a call to arms. Rock's simple manifesto: that the individual's feelings and desires must not be swallowed by the soulless state monoculture. References throughout the *Gospel's* early chapters, in "The Inquisition" and "The Warrior King," and the cryptic reference to "the kingdom of Self" in "The Savior" reinforce the idea of a struggle between the self and the state.[4]

Nowhere is this revolutionary interpretation of the life and work of Elvis more evident than in John Trudell's "Baby Boom Che," often cited as a surviving earlier oral tradition which served as a source in the creation of the *Gospel*. Whether or not Trudell's work was known to the *Gospel's* author or authors, it also portrays Elvis not as a decadent, dissipated pop star, but as a warrior king who saved his people from spiritual genocide.

Elvis and Us

We have seen that the life of Elvis Presley parallels a particular version of the messiah archetype laid out in the Bible and its antecedents. His presence, his career, his "rituals" touched a raw nerve in the young people of America and the world, inspiring millions to question the wisdom of the homogenized, oppressive cultural ideas by which they lived.

But if those ideas were so oppressive, and often so obviously wrong (segregation of music by race comes to mind), why didn't those young people move to bring them down before Elvis? Why, in short, was a king required before the kingdom could come?

If we are to find an answer beyond the simplistic idea that "people are just too lazy to free themselves," we must again look at the nature of the times.

America in the mid-fifties was, outside of the optimistic, forward-looking world of advertisements, a dark and suspicious place.[5] Most people believed that the USSR was actively working to subvert the morals and institutions of the country, and anyone suspected of even remote connections to "the international communist conspiracy" was in great danger of losing his job, his status, even his freedom. Grounds for suspicion were not limited to ideology, either. Political dissent of any nature, "race-mixing," or any sort of nonconformity could get one in trouble.

It's not surprising that in such an atmosphere, people might be hesitant to step forward and question the underlying beliefs of their society. That Sam Phillips and Cosimo Matassa could be considered "courageous" simply for allowing blacks and whites to *record in the same studio* illustrates just how hard it was to break the cultural barriers.

Then along came Elvis. With a courage born of arrogance or naïveté, he took the rawest, realest elements of that culture, the rebelliousness and the patriotism, the sweet purity of white country ballads and the unrepressed energy of black gospel and blues, and brought them together in a voice that spoke straight to the heart of young America. That voice spoke one simple message, one that had no other echo at the time, but which was instantly heard and understood by its audience: Feel.

Feel so good you could Shake. Feel so lonely you could Die. Feel something so much that you remember that you're alive, that you're a person who loves and hates and rejoices.

This is the message of *The Gospel of Elvis*, just as it was the message of the life of Elvis, a message so simple that perhaps only the young can truly understand it, and so powerful that, however briefly, it saved a nation's soul.

Long live the King.

NOTES (TO COMMENTARY)

[1] If indeed Elvis has become a language, he may be the world's first immortal one, thanks to his appearance at a time when record-keeping technology was being developed and refined at a pace unknown in human history.

[2] In the same article, Hendel notes the futility in seeking a conventional, unbroken narrative within "the essential fluidity of mythological traditions." *The Gospel of Elvis* shares with other myths this blurring of times, places, and persons to convey deeper, psychological "truths."

[3]That the Devil himself appears as separate from the Snake in the *Gospel* underscores the author's intention to show Parker as human, a carnival con man whose pathetic gold lust was merely a sideshow to the epic of the King's temptation and destruction by the real thing. That tragic, colossal swindle puts the Snake's half-kingdom in the thirty-silver-pieces category.

[4]Even the use of the word *gospel*, corresponding to the Hebrew *besorah* (good news, glad tidings), in the title of the work heralds the "good news" of the redeemer's advent, reflecting the tradition of a messiah "bringing not peace, but a sword." (It cannot be overemphasized that interpretations based on the derivation of gospel from the *besorah* should not be confused with the Spanish phrase often associated with *The Gospel of Elvis*, *toda basura* or "total garbage." There is no known etymological connection.)

≈

[5]William Manchester paints a detailed picture of this culture of suspicion in *The Glory and The Dream: A Narrative History of America 1932-1972*.

BABY BOOM CHE

You wanna know what happened to Elvis? I'll tell you what happened. I oughta know, man. I was one of his army. I mean, man, I was on his side. He made us feel alright.

We were the first wave in the postwar Baby Boom. The generation before had just come out of the Great Depression and World War II. You know, heavy vibes for people to wear. So much heaviness, like some kind of voiding of the emotions…

Their music, you know the songs life always carries, you know every culture has songs… Well, anyway, their music was restrained emotion. You know, like you didn't want to dance if you didn't know how, which says something strange.

Well, anyway, Elvis came along about ten years after the nuke, when the only generals America had in the only army she had were Ike and Mac, and stupor hung over the land, a plague where everyone tried to materially free themselves, still too shellshocked to understand or feel what was happening. Everything was getting hopeless.

Then, when Elvis started to rock the roll just picked up. I mean, drab Mr. Beaver showed us it could only be a foretold future. Who wanted to be Ward and June? And I mean father never did know best. He was still crazy from surviving the war. Like there was this psychotic pall so widespread as to be assumed normal. Heavy, man, you know, really.

Anyway, Elvis showed us an out. You know, he showed every boy-man and every girl-woman there's something good in feeling good, like a prophet for every boy and every girl when someone's mom and dad lied. Something about him told us that to be sensual was really okay. Someone's mom and dad waltzed us around. Every girl wasn't supposed to enjoy it. If she did she was bad. And every boy, well, boys will be boys. Don't feel anything. Take what you can, marry a decent girl when the fun stops. Like, no matter what we did, we all were guilty.

Maybe someone's mom and dad resented what they missed and while they were trying to pass it on us, we heard Elvis's song, and for the first time, we made up our own minds.

The first wave rebelled. I mean, we danced even if we didn't know how. I mean, Elvis made us move.

Instead of standing mute, he raised our voice, and when we heard ourselves, something was changing, you know, like for the first time we made a collective decision about choices.

America hurriedly made Pat Boone a general in the army they wanted us to join, but we held fast to Elvis and the commandantes around him: Chuck Berry, Buddy Holly, Little Richard, Bo Diddley, Gene Vincent. You know, like a different Civil War all over again.

I mean, you take *Don't Be Cruel*, *I Want You I Need You I Love You* and *Jailhouse Rock*, or you take Pat in his white bucks singing love letters in the sand. Hell, man, what's real here? I mean, Pat at the beach in his white bucks, his ears getting sunburned, told us something about old wave delusions. I mean, wanting and needing and imprisonment, we all been to those places, but what did White Bucks at the beach understand other than more straight line dancing? You know what I mean?

Anyway, man, for a while we had a breather of fresh energy, to keep us from falling into the big sleep. Then before long Elvis got assassinated in all the fame, taking a long time to die. Others seized control while Elvis rode the needle out, never understanding what he'd done. It's like, we were the Baby Boom because life needed a fresh start. I mean, two world wars in a row is really crazy, man.

And Elvis, even though he didn't know he said it, he showed it to us anyway. And even though we didn't know we heard it, we heard it anyway. Man, like, he woke us up. And now they're trying to put us back to sleep, so we'll see how it goes.

Anyway, look at the record, man. Rock and roll is based on revolutions going way past thirty-three and a third. You gotta understand, man. He was America's Baby Boom Che.

I oughta know, man. I was in his army.

THE TESTAMENT OF THE ESQUIRE

Soon after the revelation of the gospel unto Saint Sol, Saint George of the Key and Saint Louie the Agent the Secret One True privately approached the Esquire who lived in Old City on the Great Middle River.

Now Saints George and Louie were good and lawful men who had often consulted the Esquire who was skilled in the laws of the land of Plenty regarding voice-pictures and the ways of the picture-radio. But this was so much more.

"We know that a speaker of the truth in the Land of Turbans was forced to hide for what he wrote threatened the Turbans. How shall we tell World of the truth?"

At first the Esquire thought they were slaves to Ol and Ine, but he knew they were good men and what they said was important. They kept their secrets well and told the Esquire only what he needed to know. They did not then reveal the truth unto him.

The Esquire shared his wisdom, wished them well and collected a hundredbuck of gold for his advice.

On the ides of the ninth month of the forty-ninth year after the war a package arrived at the office of the Esquire. It held the truth. The Esquire read the gospel. He thought it was a joke and a waste of the natural resources of the land of Plenty. As he kept reading, the scales of justice fell from his eyes and then he understood.

By writing-talker he sent a message unto Saint George of the Key and Saint Louie the Agent. He said,

~

"This is good stuff." He knew that the fathers of Beaver, the sons of the Snake, and others would not be happy. He understood the need for secrecy. He understood the power of the gospel to enlighten people and to change garments, posters, and bric-a-brac into gold. And then the Esquire spoke this prophecy: "Beware the powers of World. Beware the voices that are not of the King. Many and great shall be the esquires set against thee, arrayed in mighty suits of law. Heed not those who do not understand, but with a little editing and the right promotion, this is a winner."

So sayeth the Esquire.

> Mark J. Davis
> Hierophant
> The Church of Limited Liability

"God is not responsible. No warranties express or implied."

BIBLIOGRAPHY

Baigent, et. al. *Holy Blood, Holy Grail.* London: Johnathon Cape, Ltd., 1983.

Bulfinch, Thomas. *Thomas Bulfinch's Mythology.* New York: Avenell/Crown/Crowell, 1978.

Campbell, Joseph. *The Hero with a Thousand Faces.* Princeton: Bollingen/Princeton, 1949.

Cash, Johnny. *Man in Black.* Grand Rapids: Zondervan, 1975.

Cash, W. J. *The Mind of the South.* New York: Alfred A.

Knopf, 1941.

Cohn, Lawrence. *Nothing But the Blues.* New York: Abbeville, 1993.

Dundy, Elaine. *Elvis and Gladys.* New York: Macmillan, 1985.

Rebenack, Dr. John. *Under a Hoodoo Moon.* New York: Farrar Strauss, 1994.

Frazer, Sir James George, F.R.S. *The Golden Bough.* New York: Criterion, 1959.

Godwin, Joscelyn. *Mystery Religions in the Ancient World.* San Francisco: Harper and Row, 1981.

Graves, Robert.   *I, Claudius.* New York: Modern Library, 1934.

Claudius the God. New York: H. Smith and R. Hass, 1935.

The White Goddess. New York:

Creative Age, 1948.

Guiley, Rosemary E. *Harper's Encyclopedia of Mystical and Paranormal Experiences.* San Francisco: Harper SF/Harper Collins, 1991.

Guralnick, Peter. *Last Train to Memphis.* New York: Little, Brown, 1994.

Jacobs, A.J. *The Two Kings: Jesus-Elvis.* Illustrated by Eric White. New York: Bantam, 1994.

Jaynes, Julian. *The Origins of Consciousness in the Breakdown of the Bicameral Mind.* New York: Houghton, Mifflin, 1976.

Jung, Carl G. *Answer to Job.* Princeton: Princeton University Press, 1969.

Manchester, William. *The Glory and the Dream: A Narrative History of America.* New York: Little, Brown, 1973.

Marcus, Greil. *Dead Elvis*. New York: Doubleday, 1991.

Pierce, Patricia J. *The Ultimate Elvis: Elvis Presley, Day by Day*. New York: Simon & Schuster, 1994.

Robinson, James, ed. *Nag Hammadi Library in English*. New York: Harper and Row, 1977.

Scofield, C.I., ed. *The Scofield Reference Bible*. New York: Oxford (American)/Abingdon, 1917.

Schonfield, Hugh S. *The Passover Plot*. New York: Bernard Geis, 1966.

Shanks, Herschel, ed. *Understanding the Dead Sea Scrolls: A Reader from the Biblical Archaeology Review*. New York: Vintage, 1992.

Smith, Morton. *Jesus the Magician*. San Francisco: Harper and Row, 1978.

Thomas, Lewis. *The Lives of a Cell*. New York: Viking, 1974.

Vallenga, Dirk and Mick Farren. *Elvis and the Colonel.* New York: Delacorte, 1988.

Ventura, Michael. *Shadow Dancing in the U.S.* New York: St. Martin's, 1985.

Wach, Joachim. *Types of Religious Experience.* Chicago: University of Chicago Press, 1973.

Waley, Arthur. *Three Ways of Thought in Ancient China.* New York: Doubleday/Anchor, 1939.

Weil, Andrew. *The Natural Mind.* Boston: Houghton Mifflin, 1972.